Research
Foundation
Literature Review

ESG AND RESPONSIBLE INSTITUTIONAL INVESTING AROUND THE WORLD

A Critical Review

Pedro Matos

CFA Institute
Research
Foundation

Statement of Purpose

The CFA Institute Research Foundation is a not-for-profit organization established to promote the development and dissemination of relevant research for investment practitioners worldwide.

Cover photo credit: fanjianhua / Getty Images

ISBN 978-1-944960-97-1

Contents

This publication qualifies for 2 PL credits under the guidelines of the CFA Institute Professional Learning Program.

ESG and Responsible Institutional Investing Around the World

A Critical Review

Pedro Matos
*John G. Macfarlane Family Chair and Professor of Business Administration,
Academic Director of Richard A. Mayo Center for Asset Management,
University of Virginia Darden School of Business*

Introduction

"ESG," "responsible investing," and "sustainable investing" are broad umbrella terms that refer to the incorporation of environmental, social, and governance (ESG) considerations into investors' portfolio decisions.[1] Investors typically assess ESG factors using nonfinancial data on environmental impact (e.g., carbon emissions), social impact (e.g., employee satisfaction), and governance attributes (e.g., board structure). This survey will provide more specific definitions, but generally, *responsible investors* will seek to either avoid or reduce exposure to investments that pose greater ESG risks or to influence companies in order to make them more ESG-friendly and thus generate more positive benefits for society. In this introduction, I present the major outstanding questions affecting ESG investing, which the survey seeks to answer.

ESG investing represents a growing portion of overall capital market investments. It is hard to estimate with precision the degree to which institutional assets pursue ESG strategies, but some survey estimates put the number in the tens of trillions of US dollars in assets under management (AUM). For example, the Global Sustainable Investment Alliance (2019) reported that more than US$30 trillion was managed according to responsible investment criteria worldwide in 2018. The data show that ESG investing is more pervasive in Europe, but it has grown rapidly in the United States in recent years. The US SIF Foundation's (2018) biennial report estimated US$12 trillion in AUM (up 38% from 2016) investing in ESG strategies. The Principles for Responsible Investment (PRI), the largest global network of institutional investors committed to considering ESG issues in their investment processes,

---

[1] I use "ESG," "responsible investing," and "sustainable investing" interchangeably throughout this survey.

1

had more than 2,500 signatories with over US$85 trillion in AUM at the end of 2019. The estimates, however, are much more modest if one focuses only on sustainable mutual funds and exchange-traded funds (ETFs) in the United States and Europe, with estimates typically lower than US$1 trillion.[2] But how realistic are these figures? Is ESG investing just another Wall Street fad, or are we at an inflection point representing a structural change in the way investors allocate resources?

ESG implementation has not been defined consistently, partly because ESG investing is evolving. In the asset management industry, where active management faces competitive pressure from index investing, ESG strategies have been the bright spot in terms of new funds being launched and receiving inflows (Morningstar 2019). In this context, there is concern over potential "greenwashing" or "rainbow washing"—a false or exaggerated representation regarding how well aligned investments really are with sustainability goals. Do ESG investors really "walk the (green) talk"?

On the structural side, one driving force behind the incorporation of ESG issues is societal change—for example, the transfer of wealth from baby boomers to the millennial generation and the increasing proportion of high-net-worth individuals who express a preference for allocating wealth in a more sustainable way.[3] Institutional investors act as agents for the individuals on whose behalf capital is being invested, and individual clients may demand that their capital be used to create wealth in ways that are perceived to be more sustainable over the long term. Another instigator of change is the increased investment regulation in the aftermath of the global financial crisis, such as prudential regulation affecting asset owners, stewardship codes for investment managers, and corporate disclosure rules set by governments or stock exchanges.[4] A large number of investment managers commit to such initiatives as the PRI, but the extent of actual implementation is not clear, because the large majority of asset managers do not disclose precisely how ESG factors inform their investment decisions. What are the driving forces behind the adoption of ESG investing around the world?

Investors may be motivated to incorporate ESG considerations into the investment process for financial reasons—in other words, to "do well by doing

---

[2]BlackRock estimated US$760 billion in AUM in a survey (BlackRock, "Sustainability: The Future of Investing," February 2019), and a Morningstar report applying a stricter classification of sustainable funds available to US investors identified only 351 open-end funds and ETFs, with US$161 billion in AUM at the end of 2018 (Morningstar, "Sustainable Funds U.S. Landscape Report," February 2019).

[3]U.S. Trust, "U.S. Trust Insights on Wealth and Worth" (2018).

[4]The PRI's responsible investment regulation database counts more than 500 policy interventions since the year 2000 (see www.unpri.org/sustainable-markets/regulation-map).

good"—with the expectation that ESG investing will enhance returns (for example, that stocks that rank well in ESG metrics will outperform the market). In recent years, the advent of new data has given rise to research on ESG investing. Some argue that ESG factors can drive firm value or possibly reduce firm risk in the long run. Others take a more skeptical view and argue that promoting socially responsible businesses should, at least in theory, come with an associated investment cost, even if this confers a nonfinancial benefit.

Can ESG investing really be a win–win for portfolio managers and their clients? Is it possible to "do good" and "do well" at the same time? These questions provide good reasons to take a thorough look at the current body of evidence on ESG investing and the role played by institutional investors in affecting corporate change.

I will also provide new evidence on these issues with novel data from the PRI. This survey is aimed at industry practitioners interested in a synthesis of the main ideas presented in recent academic research on ESG topics. I will examine the large-scale adoption of responsible and ESG investing by mainstream institutional investors, rather than narrowly surveying the literature on the performance of specialized ESG/SRI (socially responsible investing) strategies or ESG/CSR (corporate social responsibility) practices. I will concentrate primarily on ESG incorporation in public equities because the majority of academic research conducted up to now has focused on this area. The emphasis is on recent work, summarizing only the prior evidence that is well covered in previous academic literature surveys (which are referenced for those interested in further reading). ESG investing is a vibrant research area, which makes it difficult to comprehensively track all the current academic work. I apologize in advance to authors whose work is not covered here.[5]

The survey is organized as follows. I begin by defining ESG and then focus on climate change, the ESG issue that receives the most attention from institutional investors. I contrast regulatory efforts in the European Union with those in the United States. Historically, institutional investors have concentrated more on corporate governance (G), with their more recent focus being environmental and social (E&S) topics. Next, I provide evidence on the rise of institutional investors and the role they increasingly play in G. I review the waves of institutional shareholder activism in the United States, the role of foreign institutions in exporting G to non-US markets, and the open debate on the rising influence of the large index managers. Then, I examine in detail the E&S topics, covering both the economic theory and

---

[5]One useful tool to search for new academic work as it comes out is the PRI Academic ESG Review, available at www.unpri.org/academic-research/academic-esg-review/5024.article.

empirical evidence on whether firms that "do good, do well." I review the recent evidence on which types of institutional investors are concerned about and influence E&S firm outcomes. Given the lack of comprehensive evidence on ESG adoption, I subsequently present new evidence using PRI data. I also describe the results of two related studies on whether PRI signatory institutions "walk the ESG talk," as well as the success in corporate engagements of the PRI Collaboration Platform. Finally, I list several open questions and provide some concluding thoughts.

What Forces Are Driving ESG Investing?

Highlights from this section:

- *There is no consensus on the exact list of ESG issues and their materiality.*

- *The ESG issue that gets the most attention from institutional investors is climate change, in particular their portfolio companies' exposure to carbon risk and "stranded assets."*

- *Investors should be positioning themselves for increased regulation, with the regulatory agenda being more ambitious in the European Union than in the United States.*

Although it is widely recognized that capital markets have contributed to efficient resource allocation and wealth creation over the past century, the total value that corporations deliver to society through their products and services depends on the value created jointly by a set of stakeholders, such as workers, suppliers, and the communities in which they operate. In the last few years, awareness has increased that corporate exposure to such factors as environmental risks, social practices, and governance issues can materially affect firm value over the long term. High-profile examples of such ESG-related incidents include the 2001 Enron Corporation accounting fraud, the 2010 Deepwater Horizon oil spill, the 2015 Volkswagen emissions test cheating, and the 2018 Facebook data privacy scandal.

Many economists assert that the best solutions for addressing such externalities resulting from a firm's operations should come in the form of government policy tools, such as taxes or subsidies to mitigate detrimental impacts or to incentivize socially desirable corporate behaviors. To take environmental issues as an example, in the United States, green industrial policies include such laws as the Clean Air Act, federal tax credits for renewable energy projects, and state-level renewable energy standards. Rodrik (2014, p. 470), however, concluded that these policies are "strong in theory, ambiguous in practice." In an international context, this problem is exacerbated by the challenges of coordinating and implementing global environmental policies among national governments.[6]

In this context, a new model might be to leverage private capital to address ESG issues. In his 2020 letter to CEOs of the world's largest companies, Larry Fink (the chairman and CEO of BlackRock, the world's largest fund manager, with US$7 trillion in assets) warned that "climate change is different. Even if only a fraction of the projected impacts is realized, this is a much more structural, long-term crisis. Companies, investors, and governments must prepare for a significant reallocation of capital."[7] In the accompanying letter to BlackRock clients, the firm pledged to start considering "ESG risk with the same rigor that it analyzes traditional measures such as credit and liquidity risk."[8] As another example, Japan's Government Pension Investment Fund (GPIF), the world's largest pension fund, revised its investment principles in 2017 to incorporate ESG issues, and its chief investment officer declared that "as a universal owner, instead of trying to beat the market, our responsibility at GPIF is to make capital markets more sustainable."[9] A final example is when Norges Bank Investment Management (NBIM, the institution managing Norway's sovereign wealth fund) announced, in November 2012, its revised expectations in terms of corporate governance

---

[6]One example is the 2015 Paris Agreement on climate change mitigation. US President Barack Obama adopted the agreement by executive order in September 2016, but in June 2017, his successor, Donald Trump, announced that the United States would stop participating in the agreement. Another example is the European Emissions Trading System, the world's largest carbon trading scheme, where carbon emitters (fossil fuel energy firms or utility companies) can buy tradable permits to offset their carbon emissions. As carbon producers, they are incentivized to either cut emissions or pay for permits on the carbon exchange. The market price of a ton of carbon, however, has been too low to meaningfully address emissions.

[7]Larry Fink, "A Fundamental Reshaping of Finance," BlackRock letter to CEOs (14 January 2020).

[8]Larry Fink, "Sustainability as BlackRock's New Standard for Investing," BlackRock client letter (14 January 2020). This letter listed a number of initiatives to reduce ESG risks in active strategies (e.g., exiting thermal coal producers), increasing offerings in ESG ETFs, and joining Climate Action 100+ (a group of investors that engages with companies to align their business with the Paris Agreement).

[9]PRI, "Fiduciary Duty in the 21st Century" (2019). As a long-term, cross-generational investor, GPIF believes that failing to address ESG risks is against its fiduciary duty. It started passive investment tracking environmental indexes for equities and encouraging the portfolio companies to improve and disclose their carbon efficiency.

5

from its portfolio firms, followed by its more recent focus on environmental issues with divestments in coal and energy firms.[10]

In addition to investors pushing companies to be more responsive to ESG issues, in some cases corporations themselves are taking action. For example, an increasing number of public companies are publishing annual sustainability reports.[11] ESG issues are also making news as corporate CEOs increasingly advocate a framework to maximize total *stakeholder* value, not merely *shareholder* value. A widely circulated August 2019 memo by the Business Roundtable, the association of chief executives of leading US companies, titled "Statement on the Purpose of a Corporation," posited that shareholder value maximization is not the sole purpose of the corporation but that its purpose must include benefits to all its stakeholders (customers, suppliers, employees, and local communities).[12] Many observers expressed concerns about the sincerity of these intentions, however, because the terms of the memo often broke with the actual historical practices of the corporate signatories.[13] And the Council of Institutional Investors (CII), an association of US asset owners, criticized the statement for placing shareholders last and for referencing shareholders simply as providers of capital rather than as owners.[14] CII worried that "stakeholder governance" and "sustainability" can become hiding places for poor management.

Defining ESG. **Table 1** highlights some of the major ESG issues that companies typically face in seeking to generate long-term value. There is no consensus on the exact list of issues and their materiality, but the concern is that some of them may affect the value creation by a firm. These issues are increasingly topical because a growing portion of firm value lies in intangible

---

[10]Aguilera, Bermejo, Capapé, and Cuñat (2019) showed that when NBIM revised its expectations in terms of corporate governance (e.g., increased board accountability), the governance improved among portfolio firms in which the fund held positions, but there was no change in firms with no holdings.

[11]In 2017, 85% of S&P 500 Index companies published sustainability reports, which is up from 11% in 2011 (Governance & Accountability Institute, "Flash Report: 60% of Russell 1000® Are Publishing Sustainability Reports, G&A Institute's 2018 Inaugural Benchmark Study Shows" [2018]). ESG is still not commonly mentioned in earnings calls with investors, however. FactSet reported that only 31 of the S&P 500 companies mentioned "ESG" on Q3 2019 earnings call transcripts.

[12]See www.businessroundtable.org/business-roundtable-redefines-the-purpose-of-a-corporation-to-promote-an-economy-that-serves-all-americans.

[13]B. Ritholtz, "Stakeholder Capitalism Will Fail If It's Just Talk," *Bloomberg Opinion* (21 August 2019). L. Zingales, "Don't Trust CEOs Who Say They Don't Care about Shareholder Value Anymore," *Washington Post* (20 August 2019).

[14]CII, "Council of Institutional Investors Responds to Business Roundtable Statement on Corporate Purpose" (19 August 2019).

Table 1. Main ESG Issues

Environmental	Social	Governance
• Climate change and carbon emissions	• Workforce health and safety, diversity, and training	• Shareholder rights
• Natural resource use and energy and water management	• Customer and product responsibility	• Composition of boards of directors (independence and diversity)
• Pollution and waste	• Community relations and charitable activities	• Management compensation policy
• Ecodesign and innovation		• Fraud and bribery

assets, and many ESG issues relate to intangibles that most often are not at all reflected in traditional financial accounting statements.

The environmental (E) dimension measures a company's impact on the natural ecosystem, which comprises its emissions (e.g., greenhouse gases), the efficient use of natural resources in the production process (e.g., in terms of energy, water, or materials), pollution and waste (e.g., spills), and innovation efforts to eco design its products.

The social (S) dimension covers a company's relations with its workforce, customers, and society. It includes efforts to maintain loyal workers (e.g., employment quality, health and safety, training, and development), satisfy customers (e.g., producing quality goods and services that keep customers safe), and being a good citizen in the communities where it operates.

The governance (G) dimension captures the systems in place for management to act in the best interests of its long-term shareholders, which include safeguarding shareholder rights (e.g., limiting anti-takeover defenses), having a functioning board (e.g., with experienced, diverse, and independent members), maintaining well-designed executive compensation policies, and avoiding illegal practices, such as fraud and bribery.

A Special Focus on Climate Finance. The ESG issue receiving the majority of public attention in recent years relates to companies' exposure to climate change—that is, the observed warming of the earth since the mid-20th century. With so-called 100-year storms happening frequently and extreme temperatures affecting daily life and business operations,[15] it is no surprise that the Oxford Dictionaries named "climate emergency" as the 2019 Word of the Year.[16] In addition, the World Economic Forum (2019)

---

[15]U.S. Global Change Research Program, "Climate Science Special Report: Fourth National Climate Assessment (NCA4), Volume I" (2017).

[16]Jennifer Schuessler, "Oxford Names 'Climate Emergency' Its 2019 Word of the Year," *New York Times* (21 November 2019).

identified the top three risks as "extreme weather events," "failure of climate-change mitigation and adaptation," and "natural disasters."[17]

According to the Intergovernmental Panel on Climate Change (IPCC), average temperatures around the globe are currently about 1°C higher than preindustrial levels. The IPCC has associated the rise in average temperatures with the increase in anthropogenic greenhouse gas emissions that has occurred since the preindustrial era because of economic and population growth. Global greenhouse gas emissions continue to rise, with record emissions in 2018.[18] Climate scientists concluded that continued growth in emissions in line with historical rates could lead to the earth's warming of 1.5°C, relative to pre-industrial levels, between 2030 and 2052 (IPCC 2018). The IPCC warns that continued increases in emissions could ultimately result in irreversible long-term disruptive consequences for the planet.

Climate projections are inherently uncertain, but it is likely that climate change may result in physical risks and transition risks. Physical risks have already begun to materialize in the form of extreme weather and natural catastrophe losses that impose direct costs to property, land, or infrastructure. But there are also transition risks, because the IPCC estimates that achieving a mere 1.5°C maximum target increase in temperatures would require emissions to decrease to net zero by 2050. These transition risks range from "stranded assets" (e.g., oil and gas reserves that will remain unburned if climate change is to be limited) to climate-related financial risks that are not yet reflected in valuations of various assets (assets potentially written off entirely or reduced in value) for carbon-intensive businesses. Many policymakers, such as the outgoing governor of the Bank of England (Carney 2015), have referred to a link between climate change and risk in financial market stability. In addition to the risk of potentially stranded assets, moving toward a low-carbon economy carries adjustment costs. This adjustment may require mobilizing substantial amounts of capital to invest in climate change mitigation and adaptation to be accomplished in a short window of time. These investments include low-carbon solutions, such as renewable energy (e.g., wind farms), energy efficiency (e.g., green buildings), and sustainable transportation (e.g., electric vehicles).

Hong, Karolyi, and Scheinkman (2020) discussed the fact that few financial economists have done research on climate finance and little on the topic has been published to date in what is commonly perceived to be the top

---

[17]Swiss Re data show that global insured losses from catastrophes have risen in the last few years.

[18]Carbon Dioxide Information Analysis Center and Global Carbon Project, available at https://ourworldindata.org/co2-and-other-greenhouse-gas-emissions.

peer-reviewed finance journals. Recently, however, a number of working papers have examined carbon risk as it relates to markets. Bolton and Kacperczyk (2019) reviewed how stock returns vary with CO_2 emissions among US listed firms and concluded that carbon risk is largely already priced into markets. For all three categories of emissions (Scope 1, 2, and 3), the authors documented a positive and statistically significant effect on firms' stock returns.[19] The authors found some evidence that institutional investors implement exclusionary screening based on Scope 1 emissions in a few salient industries. Their findings are consistent with a "carbon premium" required by investors as compensation for idiosyncratic risk exposures tied to carbon emissions.[20] Ilhan, Sautner, and Vilkov (2020) tested whether climate policy uncertainty is priced in the options market. Using data from the Carbon Disclosure Project, they found that the cost of out-of-the-money put options (which offer protection against downside tail risks) is higher for firms with more carbon-intense business models, again suggesting that markets factor in companies' carbon-related risks. Other papers have focused on "decarbonizing" portfolios. Engle, Giglio, Kelly, Lee, and Stroebel (2019) showed how a dynamic portfolio strategy can be implemented that hedges risk with respect to climate change news constructed through textual analysis of *Wall Street Journal* articles. Finally, Cheema-Fox, LaPerla, Serafeim, Turkington, and Wang (2019) studied how institutional flows to decarbonization strategies relate to returns, as investors incorporate information about climate change into their investment processes.

In a particularly interesting study, Krueger, Sautner, and Starks (2020) surveyed the perceptions of more than 400 large institutional investors on matters related to climate change and their approach to considering climate risks in their investment decisions. Around 40% of respondents expected a global temperature rise by the end of the century that exceeds the 2°C target of the Paris Agreement and that climate risks, especially those related to regulation, have already started to materialize.[21] For example, the most common

---

[19]Scope 1 refers to direct emissions from production; Scope 2 refers to indirect emissions from consumption of purchased electricity, heat, or steam; and Scope 3 refers to other indirect emissions.

[20]Other recent papers have studied whether other material risks of climate change are priced. Hong, Li, and Xu (2019) examined "drought risk" for crops and food companies. Hsu, Li, and Tsou (2019) documented a "pollution premium" in the cross-section of stock returns based on EPA toxic chemical emissions. Bernstein, Gustafson, and Lewis (2019) studied the effects of sea level rise on property prices; Murfin and Spiegel (2020) found limited effects; and Baldauf, Garlappi, and Yannelis (2019) found that such effects depend on the heterogeneity of beliefs regarding global warming.

[21]For example, Article 173 of the French energy transition act required investors in the country to disclose how they deal with ESG criteria. The UK government is also exploring a mandatory requirement for pension funds to disclose climate-related risks.

9

motive provided by the investors surveyed is to protect reputational risk over the belief that climate risks affect portfolio risk and returns. Institutional investors seem to be in the early stages of incorporating climate risks into their investment processes. For example, many investors still do not incorporate even a basic approach to identify, quantify, and manage carbon and stranded asset risk. Although surveyed investors believe that equity valuations do not fully reflect climate risks, their perception of the degree of the price of overvaluations of carbon-related risks is relatively small.

A companion paper by Ilhan, Krueger, Sautner, and Starks (2019) surveyed the same institutional investors on their views on and preferences for firms' climate risk disclosures. A large majority of survey respondents believed that climate risk reporting by portfolio firms is important for their investment decisions but needs improvement in terms of quality and quantity. The authors complemented the survey analysis with archival data showing that greater institutional ownership from countries with strong environmental norms is associated with a higher propensity of firms to voluntarily disclose their carbon emissions. This finding is in line with Carney (2015, p. 9), who called for more to be done "to develop consistent, comparable, reliable and clear disclosure around the carbon intensity of different assets."

The Regulatory Environment. Most ESG/CSR reporting by US companies is voluntary, and the content of those reports is left to company discretion. Christensen, Hail, and Leuz (2019) offered a comprehensive literature review of accounting and finance academic work showing that there currently is substantial variation in CSR disclosures, reflecting the heterogeneity of firms' business activities. This situation makes objective comparisons of companies' CSR practices quite difficult. The authors discussed the challenges of a regulator creating and enforcing reporting standards. The literature surveyed by the authors suggests that increasing the quantity and quality of the CSR information would generate benefits to capital markets through greater liquidity, lower cost of capital, and better capital allocation. Prior literature also showed, however, that corporate disclosures involve proprietary and litigation costs. Mandatory CSR reporting would have implementation issues in terms of the CSR standard-setting process, the materiality of CSR disclosures, the use of boilerplate language as an avoidance tool by firms, and difficulties in enforcement. The authors speculated that a combination of private assurance with public enforcement is most likely to succeed.

Another dimension is the adoption of investor stewardship codes instructing institutional investors on their responsibilities in integrating ESG issues and monitoring their investments (OECD 2017). These codes are usually voluntary or imposed on a "comply-or-explain" basis. The first stewardship code was introduced in the United Kingdom in 2010 as a response to perceived excessive risk taking among financial firms contributing to the global financial crisis. The stewardship code aimed to create incentives for institutional owners to play a preventive role in excessive risk taking. Among other principles, it required institutional investors to monitor their investee companies, to have a clear voting policy, and to publicly disclose their stewardship and voting activities.[22] Some codes are initiated by regulators (e.g., the United Kingdom's Financial Reporting Council) and are binding, whereas others are introduced by industry bodies (e.g., the Canadian Coalition for Good Governance) and are often voluntary. There is a concern, however, that codes might be merely superficial; institutions sign up merely to "tick the box," not to truly embrace stewardship. In 2014, the Financial Reporting Council sounded an alarm: "Too many signatories fail to follow through on their commitment to the code."[23]

Different regions around the world are proceeding at different speeds on ESG regulation. The EU currently has an ambitious regulatory agenda backed by strong political support for a transition to a low-carbon economy. In 2018, the European Commission released the Action Plan: Financing Sustainable Growth, with several policy initiatives aimed at reorienting private capital toward sustainable projects so as to meet the 2030 targets that the EU committed to as part of the Paris Agreement.[24] Following the recommendations from the EU High-Level Expert Group on Sustainable Finance, the package included a taxonomy to classify sustainability activities, standards, and labels for green financial products and developing sustainability benchmarks. Other proposals included obligations for institutional investors to disclose how they integrated ESG factors into their investment process and asking investors about their ESG preferences. Some individual EU member countries have also developed their own policies, such as Article 173 of the

---

[22]The new version of the UK Stewardship Code took effect on 1 January 2020 and revises the latest update, from 2012 (see www.frc.org.uk/investors/uk-stewardship-code). The introduction of the 2012 code stated, "For investors, stewardship is more than just voting. Activities may include monitoring and engaging with companies on matters such as strategy, performance, risk, capital structure, and corporate governance, including culture and remuneration. Engagement is purposeful dialogue with companies on these matters as well as on issues that are the immediate subject of votes at general meetings."

[23]Financial Reporting Council, "Developments in Corporate Governance and Stewardship 2014" (2015).

[24]European Commission, "Sustainable Finance." https://ec.europa.eu/info/business-economy-euro/banking-and-finance/sustainable-finance_en.

French Energy Transition for Green Growth Law, which asked fund managers to develop sustainability and decarbonization policies.[25]

In the United States, the regulatory environment is not yet settled. For example, the regulatory environment regarding pension plans reflects the nation's current partisan divide, with an active debate on whether fiduciary duties of loyalty and prudence should include the consideration of ESG factors. Standards for "fiduciary duties" require institutional investors to invest their beneficiaries' funds prudently and in the best interest of the client. The decision on whether to integrate ESG factors into this duty depends on whether it is believed that these factors materially affect portfolio performance (consistent with the duty of care) and the well-being of beneficiaries (consistent with the duty of loyalty). Starting with the Employee Retirement Income Security Act of 1974 (ERISA), the US Department of Labor (DOL) noted in different bulletins that fiduciaries should not sacrifice the economic interests of pension plan participants to promote ESG goals. It relaxed this guidance under the Obama administration in 2015, when it clarified that ESG criteria could be used in a fiduciary's investment framework. In 2018, however, under the Trump administration, the DOL reaffirmed that fiduciaries "must avoid too readily treating ESG issues as being economically relevant. . . . Rather, ERISA fiduciaries must always put first the economic interests of the plan in providing retirement benefits."[26]

The SEC also has no clear regulatory priority on ESG issues. The current SEC chair has emphasized that investment advisers cannot put any interests, including ESG factors, ahead of those of their clients.[27] The SEC's approach seems limited to improving disclosure for the investor to make informed choices. For ESG-labeled mutual funds, there are reports that in 2019 the SEC Office of Compliance Inspections and Examinations sent exam request letters to firms related to their ESG scoring systems, investment decisions, and ESG-related marketing materials.[28] At the state level, one example is California Senate Bill 964, which was signed into law in 2018 and requires the nation's two largest pension funds (CalSTRS and CalPERS) to assess the climate-related financial risks of their public market portfolios beginning in 2020.

---

[25]PRI, "French Energy Transition Law: Global Investor Briefing on Article 173" (22 April 2016).

[26]DOL, "U.S. Department of Labor Releases Field Assistance Bulletin Clarifying Issues Regarding Proxy Voting, Shareholder Engagement, and Economically Targeted Investments" (23 April 2018).

[27]Jay Clayton, "SEC Chairman Remarks to the SEC Investor Advisory Committee" (13 December 2018).

[28]Juliet Chung and Dave Michaels, "ESG Funds Draw SEC Scrutiny," *Wall Street Journal* (16 December 2019).

Regulatory approaches vary across other regions of the world. For example, China issued the "Guidelines for Establishing the Green Financial System" in August 2016, whereas Japan's approach has been to promote voluntary adoption of disclosure practices. But given how the world has globalized, Europe's more ambitious regulatory efforts (in terms of product labelling, corporate disclosure, and taxonomy) will likely affect investment managers in other regions and be the biggest driver of the growth of sustainable investment.

What Role Can Institutional Investors Play in Corporate Governance?

Highlights from this section:

- *Institutional investors are now the largest holders of shares in public companies around the world.*

- *The value of good corporate governance is "top of mind" for institutional investors, but there is a continued debate on its proper measurement.*

- *In the United States, the first waves of institutional shareholder activism had limited success, but there is stronger evidence that the last decade of hedge fund activism has had an effect.*

- *Outside the United States, the rise of foreign institutional ownership has led to the convergence of corporate governance practices of firms around the world to the US shareholder-centric model.*

- *One of the most hotly debated topics is the increase in indexed investment strategies and the rising influence of the "Big Three" index fund managers.*

The Rise of Institutional Investors Worldwide. Institutional investors increasingly play a crucial capital allocation role in modern capital markets. By institutional investors, I mean professional investors who invest growing pools of capital on behalf of their ultimate beneficiaries or individual clients.[29]

---

[29]Institutional investors are typically classified into six groups: (1) bank asset management divisions; (2) insurance companies; (3) investment companies (mutual fund families); (4) investment advisers; (5) pension funds (public or private, defined benefit or defined contribution), endowments (academic institutions or private foundations), and sovereign wealth funds; and (6) hedge funds and others.

13

A recent report by the OECD (2019) showed that as a group, institutional money managers control more than 40% of public equity market capitalization worldwide as of year-end 2017.[30]

Figure 1 shows that the importance of this group of investors varies across individual markets. It is highest in the United States and the United Kingdom, where institutional investors hold around 72% and 63%, respectively, of outstanding shares of their respective domestic stock markets.[31] In most of continental Europe and the rest of the world, other categories of shareholders still hold large stakes and retail ownership is also quite relevant.[32] One of the reasons behind the rise of institutional ownership is the reforms of pension systems from "pay as you go" to funded and defined contribution pension plans, which have been increasingly adopted around the world (OECD 2019). With institutional investors now holding collectively the largest stakes in public companies around the world, their focus on ESG issues is worthy of examination.

Does Corporate Governance Matter for Firm Value? In many ways, the "G" in "ESG" is not new. In their survey on corporate governance, Shleifer and Vishny (1997, p. 737) defined corporate governance as "the ways in which suppliers of finance to corporations assure themselves of getting a return on their investment." The authors provided an overview of the fundamental principal–agent problem, commonly referred to as the separation of ownership and control, going back at least to Berle and Means (1932) or perhaps Adam Smith (1776).[33] When a firm's managers are distinct from its

---

[30]Institutional investors are required to file their equity portfolio holdings in many countries. For example, in the United States, institutional investment managers that exercise investment discretion over $100 million or more must report their holdings of equity-like securities on Form 13F with the SEC. More details on FactSet Ownership data can be found in Ferreira and Matos (2008).

[31]Institutional ownership has risen dramatically in the US market, from only 6% of outstanding equity in 1950 (Conference Board, "The 2010 Institutional Investment Report: Trends in Asset Allocation and Portfolio Composition," 2010). Gompers and Metrick (2001) is one of the first papers to examine 13F filings to investigate the rise of "large" institutional investors in the US market in the 1980s and 1990s.

[32]Although this survey focuses on institutional ownership, OECD (2019) also highlighted that another major shareholder is public sector ownership, representing 14% of global stock market capitalization, especially in emerging market economies, such as China, Brazil, India, and Russia. Hsu, Liang, and Matos (2018) showed that state-owned enterprises (which they referred to as "Leviathan Inc.") engage more in environmental issues than non-state-owned enterprises.

[33]Smith (1776), in *The Wealth of Nations*, criticized the joint-stock company: "The directors of such companies, however, being the managers rather of other people's money than of their own, it cannot well be expected, that they should watch over it with the same anxious vigilance with which the partners in a private copartnery frequently watch over their own."

Figure 1. Percentage of Market Capitalization Owned by Category of Investor, December 2017

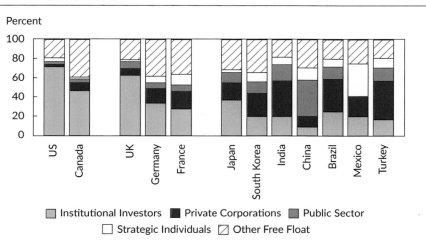

Sources: OECD (2019) statistics are constructed using firm-level ownership data from FactSet Ownership.

ultimate owners, managers may have reduced incentives to maximize firm value. This notion has been at the core of corporate finance theory since at least the Jensen and Meckling (1976) theory of the agency costs of outside equity. The classical examples include executive perks, such as corporate jets (Yermack 2006), "empire-building" (Jensen 1986), or enjoying the benefits of a so-called quiet life (Bertrand and Mullainathan 2003). Shleifer and Vishny (1997) presented extensive evidence of agency costs and differences in corporate governance systems around the world related to the level of legal protection of investor rights. The authors explained that concentrated ownership is a way to help investors "get their money back," but these large shareholders may also seek ways to redistribute wealth from minority shareholders to themselves.

I will also refer interested readers to three other surveys for a comprehensive overview of the first generation of academic research on corporate governance. The first, by Becht, Bolton, and Röell (2003), covers in depth the theoretical models and empirical evidence on alternative corporate governance mechanisms: (1) partial concentration of ownership and control in the hands of a few large investors; (2) hostile takeovers and proxy voting contests, which concentrate ownership and/or voting power temporarily; (3) delegation and concentration of control in the board of directors; (4) alignment of managerial interests with investors through executive compensation contracts; and

(5) fiduciary duties for CEOs together with class action suits. The second, by Denis and McConnell (2003), offers a more international overview, covers the differences that non-US companies have vis-à-vis a typical large US corporation in terms of both internal governance mechanisms (e.g., more concentrated ownership and separating control from cash flow rights) and external mechanisms (e.g., the importance of the legal system), and discusses the convergence of governance systems to the US model. The third, by Claessens and Yurtoglu (2013), offers a helpful survey of corporate governance in emerging market economies.

In an influential article, Gompers, Ishii, and Metrick (2003) took an investor rights perspective with a first examination of the equity value consequences of corporate governance for US firms. The authors combined individual elements of the power-sharing rules between investors and managers into a single metric or overall rating of a firm's governance. Their governance index (G-index) is based on the number of provisions that restrict shareholder rights (increase managerial power) and consists of 24 provisions tracked by the Investors Responsibility Research Center. These provisions include tactics to delay hostile bids (e.g., classified board), voting rights (e.g., supermajority), director/officer protection (e.g., golden parachutes), other takeover defenses (e.g., poison pills), and state laws (e.g., business combination laws). The study developed a governance-based trading strategy and found that S&P 1500 firms with higher G-index values (poorer governance) realized lower average future returns during the 1990s. The authors further documented a positive association between shareholder-friendly governance and firm valuation (Tobin's q ratios). The combination of high valuation ratios and higher future excess returns for firms with stronger governance suggests that the value of corporate governance is not fully priced in by investors.

Outside the United States, Aggarwal, Erel, Stulz, and Williamson (2009) constructed a firm-level governance index (GOV) using 44 governance attributes for non-US firms and found that these firms generally have a lower GOV value than US firms, suggesting that non-US firms generally provide less power to minority shareholders. The authors further concluded that the value of non-US firms falls as their GOV level decreases relative to an index of matching US firms. Both Aggarwal et al. (2009) and Gompers et al. (2003) are commonly cited as evidence that good governance matters for equity shareholders.

These original studies were followed by considerable academic inquiry. For example, Bebchuk, Cohen, and Ferrell (2009) showed that the Gompers et al. (2003) results were driven by 6 out of the 24 provisions, and they constructed an entrenchment index (E-Index). Bebchuk et al. (2009) argued that only six key provisions (staggered board, limits on amending bylaws, limits on amending the charter, supermajority to approve a merger, golden parachutes, and poison pills) were considered by legal scholars and merger and acquisition (M&A) practitioners to have real significance.[34] The authors also criticized the potential measurement error resulting from the "kitchen sink" governance indexes that use a large number of governance attributes subsequently developed by proxy adviser and corporate governance rating firms (e.g., Institutional Shareholder Services). These governance ratings were used as guides in organizing firms' governance arrangements.[35] Institutional investors began to use such ratings as "red flags" (in order to identify firms in their portfolio that require added attention for potential risks) and as inputs into tradable indexes (e.g., the FTSE ISS Corporate Governance Index Series). However, Daines, Gow, and Larcker (2010) examined widely available commercial corporate governance rankings and found that these backward-looking indicators had little power in predicting governance-related outcomes, such as accounting restatements and shareholder litigation.

The empirical link between G and shareholder returns during the 1990s did not hold in the 2000s, according to Bebchuk, Cohen, and Wang (2013). The authors interpreted their findings as investors learning to properly price the differences between well-governed and poorly governed firms. The idea is that with the increased academic research and media articles about governance, trading on the basis of G information might have subsequently stopped yielding abnormal returns. The authors further found, however, that governance indexes remain associated with firm value and operating performance. This finding suggests that investors in recent years have properly priced good governance, rewarding high-G firms with higher market valuations and a lower cost of capital, but there are no longer surprises in the form of future abnormal returns.

Some academics have raised concerns regarding the idea of the "one-size-fits-all" global governance standards—that is, whether a single set of criteria

---

[34]In a related study, Cremers and Ferrell (2014) hand-collected out-of-sample data that tracked restrictions on shareholder rights back to 1978 and documented that the negative association between restrictions on shareholder rights and Tobin's q appeared only after the 1985 landmark Delaware Supreme Court decision of *Moran v. Household*, resolving substantial legal uncertainty concerning the use of anti-takeover defenses.

[35]The development of these indexes might also put pressure on firms to change their governance arrangements in ways that would improve their rankings. The US Government Accountability Office (GAO) conducted a study of potential conflicts, but it was satisfied that proxy advisory and governance ratings firms had taken appropriate steps to prevent abuse. GAO, "Report to Congressional Requesters: Corporate Shareholder Meetings; Issues Relating to Firms That Advise Institutional Investors on Proxy Voting" (June 2007).

can be used to evaluate firm-level governance around the world—namely, the indexes of protection of investor rights described previously (G-index, E-index, and GOV) and also used by corporate governance rating firms. Bebchuk and Hamdani (2009) argued that it depends on whether the main conflict is between management and shareholders (common in US/Anglo-Saxon markets) or between controlling shareholders and minority shareholders (more prominent in non-US markets). In an examination of emerging market firms, Black, De Carvalho, and Gorga (2012) argued that "good" governance practices depend importantly on country characteristics. In addition, the history of corporate governance scandals and the 2008 global financial crisis have led others to raise concerns about G that is too strong. Admati (2017) warned that "financialized" corporate governance might incentivize managers to commit fraud or misallocate resources through short-termism or mismanagement of risk. This scenario is a special concern for banks and other financial firms, wherein the downside risk might harm shareholders and the broader economy.

Institutional Investors' Activism on Corporate Governance. The rise in importance of institutional investors has disrupted the paradigm of the widely dispersed shareholder ownership model of the publicly listed firm (Berle and Means 1932), with most corporations now having a substantial portion of their shares held by a smaller number of shareholders. Institutional investors offer the opportunity to pool assets, invest on a large scale, and reduce the principal–agent problem of dispersedly held firms with many retail investors—each of them "atomistic" and subject to the Grossman and Hart (1980) free-rider problem. Also, because active investors incur all the costs (while the benefits accrue to all shareholders), only institutions with relatively large positions can obtain a sufficient return on their investment to justify the costs of active ownership (Shleifer and Vishny 1986). Dissatisfied with some aspect of a company's management, institutions can attempt to bring about change either through "voice" (e.g., quiet diplomacy in persuading management, intervening directly by voting their shares or engaging in confrontational proxy fights) or by threatening to "exit" (e.g., selling and depressing stock prices, also known as "voting with their feet" or the "Wall Street walk" rule). Managers could be rewarded with a loyal shareholder base if institutional investors are satisfied.

The academic literature on the potential governance role played by large shareholders (known as outside "blockholders" and hereafter referred to as such) is considerable. Edmans (2014) offered a good survey of the theoretical models on blockholders: theories of voice/intervention, exit/trading, and the potential costs of blockholders.[36] He also discussed the empirical challenges of identifying which firms attract blockholders and the impact of blockholder presence or actions on firm outcomes. Identifying causal effects is difficult either in isolating a source of exogenous variation in the independent variable of interest or because many actions are typically unobservable. Focusing on the institutional ownership literature, one instrumental variable commonly used is the addition of a stock to the S&P 500 (e.g., Aghion, Van Reenen, and Zingales 2013) or the MSCI ACWI Index (e.g., Ferreira and Matos 2008).[37] One solution to the unobservable actions problem is to survey block-holders directly on the governance mechanisms they use behind the scenes (as in the clinical study of the Hermes UK Focus Fund by Becht, Franks, Mayer, and Rossi [2009] or the investor survey by McCahery, Sautner, and Starks [2016]).

Although institutional investors represent a large proportion of the overall market, the question remains: To what extent do they affect corporate governance in the interest of shareholders? The modern notion of shareholder activism began in the mid-1980s with the creation of the Council of Institutional Investors by public pension funds, continued in the mid-1990s with shareholder proposals from union funds, and started to include more mainstream investors in the 2000s. Gillan and Starks (2007) reviewed the historical evolution of shareholder activism in the US market and its link to the growing role of institutional investors. The authors showed the evolution of shareholder proposals and provided a survey the of the literature; although some studies found positive short-term market reactions to announcements of certain kinds of activism, evidence for improvement in the long term was more limited. It was also difficult to establish a causal relationship between shareholder activism and such changes. The review by Yermack (2010) on the topic of shareholder voting also found only a limited effect of shareholder activism. More recently, Denes, Karpoff, and McWilliams (2017) synthesized the results of more than 70 studies and documented that although activism had few consequential effects in the 1980s and 1990s, in the 2000s a new strain of shareholder activism sponsored by hedge funds was more associated with value improvements.

---

[36]For a longer survey, see Edmans and Holderness (2017).

[37]This identification strategy is not without critics, because inclusion in the S&P 500 might convey positive information (e.g., Denis, McConnell, Ovtchinnikov, and Yu 2003). More-recent studies have identified the effect of institutional investors on firm outcomes by comparing firms that lie close to either side of the Russell 1000 Index/Russell 2000 Index threshold using regression discontinuity designs, but there is also an active debate about this "quasi-experiment" being suitable to identify the overall effect of institutional ownership (Glossner 2018; Wei and Young 2019).

What can we learn from this new wave of hedge fund activism? Brav, Jiang, and Kim (2015) provided a review of the literature. The authors reported that by the mid-2000s, more than 150 activist hedge funds were active each year, advocating for changes in more than 200 publicly listed companies in the United States. The authors hand-collected a comprehensive sample of more than 2,600 activism events in the United States from 1994 to 2011 from regulatory filings (SEC Schedule 13D filings that are mandatory when a shareholder acquires 5% or more of a public company) and news searches. The authors documented positive abnormal returns around the disclosure of the activist position and real and long-term effects in terms of firm productivity. Becht, Franks, Grant, and Wagner (2017) extended the evidence internationally. Hedge fund engagement outcomes (such as board changes and takeovers) vary across countries and contribute to the returns to activism. Japan, however, is an exception, with high initial expectations and low outcomes. The authors showed that the increase in US foreign institutional holdings has significantly contributed to hedge fund activism becoming a global phenomenon.

There has also been skepticism about the potential governance role that institutional investors can realistically play in being effective change agents. The concern is that the rise of institutional investors might actually be increasing the distance between savers and companies. Investment managers themselves are prone to agency problems, and Gilson and Gordon (2013) referred to the conflicts between the interests of fund managers and investors as the "agency costs of agency capitalism." For example, institutions may not be the best corporate monitors if their business model involves having as customers some of the corporations whose shares they hold in their portfolio—for example, by running their employee benefit plans, such as 401(k) plans. Davis and Kim (2007) found that mutual fund families with business ties are more likely to vote with the management of client firms. Bebchuk, Cohen, and Hirst (2017) argued that the incentive structure of the fund management industry may lead to the passivity of institutional investors, which I will cover in more detail later.

The Special Role of Foreign Institutional Investors. With the rise of globalization and the elimination of explicit barriers to cross-border investment, capital has begun to flow more easily internationally instead of being saved and invested in the same country. Mutual funds, pension funds, and other vehicles offer a chance for households to diversify their portfolios across a wider set of markets than retail investors could do by themselves. In recent decades, as markets became more globalized, there has been a significant

Figure 2. Percentage of Market Capitalization Owned by Foreign Institutional Investors, December 2017

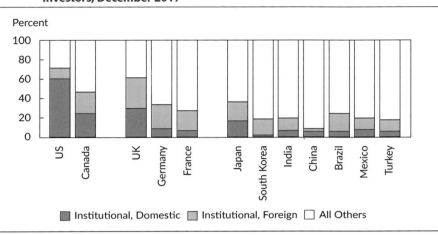

Sources: OECD (2019) statistics are constructed using firm-level ownership data from FactSet Ownership.

increase in ownership by foreign institutional investors. **Figure 2** shows how the fraction held by foreign institutions varies around the world.

Globally, US-domiciled institutional investors occupy a dominant position with respect to the total value of equity holdings—accounting for about two-thirds of global equity holdings—and hold a significant percentage of outstanding shares in most other stock markets (OECD 2019). **Figure 3** illustrates the distribution of institutional holdings among domestic institutions, US-domiciled foreign institutions, and non-US foreign institutions.

In an early survey on institutional investor monitoring, Gillan and Starks (2003) described how foreign institutions could potentially take a relatively more active role in the corporate governance of firms around the world. Together with Miguel Ferreira and other co-authors, I have conducted a number of studies examining whether foreign institutions can actually act as outside monitors and better push for shareholder value creation. We used the same institutional ownership data from FactSet Ownership as the OECD (2019) statistics used in the figures presented previously.[38]

In the first published study, we showed that the "color of money" matters (Ferreira and Matos 2008). We examined institutional investor clienteles

---

[38]The FactSet Ownership data are available to other academic researchers (upon subscription) via Wharton Research Data Services at http://wrds-web.wharton.upenn.edu/wrds/ds/factset/holdingsbyfirmmsci/index.cfm.

21

Figure 3. Percentage of Market Capitalization Owned by US Foreign Institutional Investors, December 2017

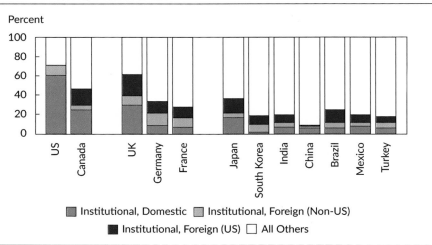

Percent

Sources: OECD (2019) statistics are constructed using firm-level ownership data from FactSet Ownership.

in terms of their geographical origin (e.g., foreign versus domestic) and in terms of any potential business ties with the firms in which they invest (e.g., "independent" mutual fund managers versus "grey" institutions, such as bank trusts). We found that firms with higher ownership by foreign (particularly US) and independent institutions have higher valuations and better operating performance. We concluded that the "colors" of investors matter in terms of monitoring corporate managers' decisions.

Is there any evidence that this phenomenon is the result of improved G? In a follow-up study, we found that foreign institutions are influential in global markets by facilitating cross-border M&A transactions and building bridges across firms in their portfolio. In Ferreira, Massa, and Matos (2010), we uncovered evidence that foreign institutional ownership is positively associated with the intensity of cross-border M&A activity worldwide. This finding is consistent with foreign portfolio investors, less encumbered by ties with management than domestic institutions, facilitating cross-border M&A activity by reducing bargaining and transaction costs. We documented that foreign institutional ownership increases the probability that a merger deal is cross-border and successful.

Building on the prior two papers, my co-authors and I explored whether foreign institutional investors might be effective in helping "export" US-style shareholder-centric governance practices to corporations located elsewhere.

Fellow researchers had developed the governance index (GOV) in Aggarwal et al. (2009) that I highlighted previously. In Aggarwal, Erel, Ferreira, and Matos (2011), we established a link between international portfolio investment and the adoption of better corporate governance practices that promote corporate accountability and empower shareholders. We documented that changes in institutional ownership over time positively affect subsequent changes in firm-level governance (e.g., board independence, audit committee, unification of share classes, and executive stock incentive plans). We also provided evidence that institutional ownership has a direct effect on terminating poorly performing CEOs. Our findings showed that market forces can promote good corporate governance practices around the world.

In a related study, my co-authors and I documented this convergence, particularly in executive pay practices between CEOs in US firms and their foreign counterparts. One of the most widely accepted "stylized facts" in the literature is that CEOs in the United States are paid significantly more than their counterparts in other countries. Attempts to study the magnitude and determinants of the US pay premium, however, had been plagued by international differences in the disclosure of CEO pay. In Fernandes, Ferreira, Matos, and Murphy (2013), we conducted a comprehensive study of CEO pay among firms in 14 countries with mandated disclosure rules. We showed that the US pay premium is economically modest after controlling for differences in ownership and governance and that the premium reflects the performance-based compensation demanded by institutional shareholders and independent boards of the more widely held US firms. We also showed that non-US CEO pay has largely converged for firms exposed to US capital, product, and labor markets.

The final paper in the series, Bena, Ferreira, Matos, and Pires (2017), tackled the issue of to what extent foreign investors have led firms to adopt a short-term orientation at the expense of forgoing long-term positive-return investments. Our results run contrary to the popular perception of non-domestic money managers as "locusts" (for what is often viewed as their plaguing effect on local companies by media and politicians). Instead, we found that higher foreign institutional ownership leads to more long-term investment in capital expenditures, R&D, and human capital. Foreign institutional ownership also leads to a significant increase in innovation output (in terms of patents), as well as to increases in the internationalization of a firm's operations and firm valuation. We showed that these effects are explained by the disciplinary and monitoring roles of foreign institutions. We identified these effects by exploiting the exogenous increase in foreign institutional ownership that follows the addition of a stock to the MSCI ACWI indexes (which are used as benchmarks by foreign investors but, importantly, not by domestic investors).

In sum, this group of studies suggests that the trend toward globalization of firms' shareholder structures resulting from increasing cross-border portfolio flows by institutional investors has led to the convergence of corporate governance practices around the world and thus represents a positive force for long-term efficient capital formation. Foreign institutional investors tend to be the agents in this change, playing a prominent role as active shareholders worldwide and replacing the model of concentrated ownership historically predominant outside the United States.

The Emerging Role of the "Big Three." For many public corporations, a substantial proportion of their shares are now held by a small number of institutional investors. **Figure 4** shows that the highest level of concentration is observed in the United States, where the three largest institutional investors hold 25% of the capital in listed companies in the OECD (2019) report.

This phenomenon is associated with the increasing use of indexed, or passive, investment strategies by investors. The index fund market is dominated by three investment managers—BlackRock, Vanguard, and State Street (sometimes referred to as the "Big Three")—that manage the majority of indexed funds. The move toward index funds is driven by the growing recognition of their low costs and the evidence that indexing outperforms most actively managed equity funds (French 2008). This inflow into index funds and ETFs has accelerated since the global financial crisis, and the phenomenon is most

Figure 4. Percentage of Market Capitalization Owned by Top Three Institutional Investors, December 2017

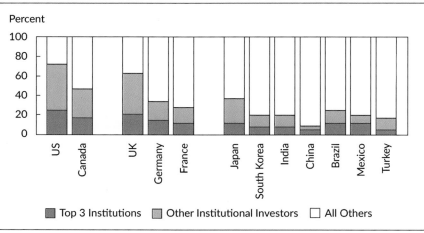

Sources: OECD (2019) statistics are constructed using firm-level ownership data from FactSet Ownership.

pronounced in the United States, but it is spreading globally.[39] According to BlackRock (2017), indexed investments accounted for 17.5% in global equity market investments in 2017, and Sushko and Turner (2018) estimated that the share of indexed equity funds in equity funds globally was around 37% in 2017, up from 15% in 2007.

What are the consequences of the Big Three for G? This topic of current academic research is hotly debated. The reason that index managers might matter is through the "voice" mechanism I outlined previously, because these managers cannot "vote with their feet," and so "if you can't sell, you must care." Index investors could be the providers of long-term capital that will stick with the portfolio firms through good times and bad. The Big Three are increasingly visible and may come under increasing reputational and regulatory pressure to be good stewards of capital. At the time of writing this survey, the cover page of *Bloomberg Businessweek* was "Total World Domination: The Index Funds in Your Piggy Bank Are Great Investments. But at What Cost?" (13 January 2020 issue).

So are passive investors also passive owners, or are they actually active blockholders? The answer remains unresolved. Appel, Gormley, and Keim (2016) showed that the increase in ownership by passive mutual funds associated with stock reassignment from the Russell 1000 Index to the Russell 2000 Index leads to governance improvements (e.g., more independent directors, fewer takeover defenses, more equal voting rights). In their follow-up work, Appel, Gormley, and Keim (2018) found that greater passive ownership is associated with greater success by hedge fund activists in obtaining board representation, removing takeover defenses, and facilitating the sale of a targeted company. However, Schmidt and Fahlenbrach (2017) found contradicting evidence in that increases in passive ownership are associated with fewer new independent director appointments, and Heath, Macciocchi, Michaely, and Ringgenberg (2020) documented that index funds are more likely to vote in accordance with a firm's management recommendations. In addition, Brav, Jiang, Li, and Pinnington (2018) found that active funds are significantly more pro-dissident than passive funds in supporting activist shareholders in proxy contests (a subset of shareholder proposals). Iliev, Kalodimos, and Lowry (2018) examined data on investor views of SEC EDGAR company

---

[39]Investment Company Institute (2019) showed that from 2009 through 2018, indexed US domestic equity mutual funds and ETFs received $1.6 trillion in flows, while actively managed domestic equity mutual funds experienced net outflows. The competitive pressure from index funds and ETFs (for which the average expense ratios fell from 0.27% in 2000 to 0.08% in 2018) has led to fee compression also for actively managed equity mutual funds (from 1.06% to 0.76% during the same period).

filings and found that relative to active funds, index funds conduct significantly less research on their portfolio firms. These last four papers would then suggest that passive investors are currently also passive monitors.

Research into index funds' monitoring is still ongoing, but two opposing views have emerged:

1. The Big Three do too little: This view is based on the idea that index managers are "lazy" passive owners and have little incentive to devote resources to monitoring companies because they compete on fees and their primary objective is to match the performance of indexes at low cost. Facing cost pressures, these institutional investors are incentivized to limit spending on global stewardship activities and may even face political or business backlash if they become too involved in publicly opposing corporate management. Bebchuk and Hirst (2019) reviewed the arguments for why the Big Three might underinvest in stewardship and be excessively deferential to the managers of portfolio companies in their proxy voting. They then examined actual stewardship investments and concluded that the Big Three have limited governance personnel, engage only a small fraction of portfolio companies, exhibit pro-management voting, and stay on the sidelines of governance reforms or security litigation.[40]

2. The Big Three do too much: This opposite view builds on the concern that with index funds being invested across various firms within the same industry, they could have incentives to encourage those corporations to engage in anticompetitive behavior that would enable them to capture monopolistic rents. In one of the first studies, Azar, Schmalz, and Tecu (2018) argued that "common ownership" (the fact that many competitor companies are jointly held by a small set of large institutional investors) causes higher seat ticket prices in the US airline industry. The authors used BlackRock's acquisition of Barclays Global Investors to obtain quasi-exogenous variation in common ownership. Coates (2018) warned about the "problem of 12"—that in the near future, 12 individual asset management firms could have practical power over the majority of US public companies. Common ownership has generated considerable media attention and led to public hearings at the US Federal Trade Commission and OECD.[41] There has

---

[40]However, Morningstar (2017) showed that the top active fund families have even smaller stewardship teams, do less private engagements, and have voting behavior that is not much different from that of the Big Three.

[41]BlackRock has been the most vocal and created a dedicated website identifying the faulty assumptions and problematic data and providing a replication package for the Azar et al. (2018) study: www.blackrock.com/common-ownership.

been an active academic debate about the appropriateness of the approach and empirical measures used in the Azar et al. (2018) study, and thus about the robustness of the conclusions and their applicability to other industries (Dennis, Gerardi, and Schenone 2019; Gilje, Gormley, and Levit 2019), as well as the identification strategy (Lewellen and Lowry 2019).

So, do the Big Three do enough, too much, or too little? A lack of academic consensus remains, and it might just be too early to tell. Still, this structural change in public equity markets—the Big Three crowding out the active managers—will likely be the subject of much more academic inquiry.

What Role Can Institutional Investors Play in E&S/CSR Issues?

Highlights from this section:

- *There is an active theoretical debate on the value of CSR for firms.*

- *There is no clear-cut empirical evidence that firms that "do good, do well"; it depends on the context.*

- *Similarly, there is no consistent evidence that SRI strategies have produced enhanced returns.*

- *Different types of institutional investors (depending on their horizon or origin) care differently about E&S outcomes, but there is growing client demand for institutional investors to care.*

Does E&S/CSR Matter? The Theory. When it comes to integrating environmental and social considerations in business operations, textbook economics has long embraced the shareholder value perspective—that the corporation exists to make money for its shareholders.[42] This perspective is based on two pillars of economic thinking: that the pursuit of self-interest by consumers and corporations results in economic efficiency (Smith 1776)

---

[42]There is some legal debate on this principle, but Delaware court decisions have established the shareholder primacy rule. According to Leo Strine, Jr., under Delaware law (where the majority of US publicly listed corporations are incorporated), directors owe their loyalty to the shareholders who elect them. As he retired, however, the Delaware Supreme Court's Chief Justice made a call for US corporate governance systems to align with ESG issues (Strine 2019).

and that the state is responsible for correcting market failures, externalities, and inequalities (Pigou 1920). The view that firms should not pursue CSR was best expressed in a 1970 *New York Times Magazine* article by Milton Friedman:

> In a free-enterprise, private-property system, a corporate executive is an employee of the owners of the business. He has a direct responsibility to his employers. That responsibility is to conduct the business in accordance with their desires, which generally will be to make as much money as possible while conforming to the basic rules of the society, both those embodied in law and those embodied in ethical custom.

For example, tax considerations aside, it is preferable that the money spent in corporate philanthropy be paid out to shareholders in the form of dividends and then allocated by them to charity as they see fit, rather than allocated to charities by corporate managers directly. Under this view, CSR is symptomatic of agency problems, with the interests of managers and shareholders in conflict with one another and with shareholders implicitly forced to contribute to charities with which they may not sympathize.

In contrast, much of the management literature has argued that a company should be accountable not just to its shareholders but also to its community, employees, and customers. This stakeholder theory was introduced by Freeman (1984) as the notion that a firm has relationships with many constituent groups (not just shareholders) that both affect and are affected by the actions of a firm.[43] McWilliams and Siegel (2001, p. 117) characterized CSR as "actions that appear to further some social good, beyond the interests of the firm and what is required by the law."

Bénabou and Tirole (2010) offered a more current view on CSR from an economist's perspective.[44] One motivation for CSR is as a response to the failure of the state (or policymakers) to correct market failures and externalities resulting from the inefficiency of governments, lobbies, or territoriality of jurisdiction. Another view of CSR might be that companies can promote values not necessarily shared by policymakers. The authors listed three ways in which CSR can affect shareholder value: (1) Firms can "do well by doing good" if they overcome managerial short-termism and reduce ESG risks (e.g., reducing workplace injury); (2) "delegated philanthropy" by firms can maximize shareholder value when they exercise pro-social behavior on behalf of

---

[43]Kitzmueller and Shimshack (2012) offered a review of the evolution of theory on the CSR topic.

[44]I chose to highlight Bénabou and Tirole (2010) and Hart and Zingales (2017), but many other economists have views on CSR. See, for example, Mayer (2013); Magill, Quinzii, and Rochet (2015); Albuquerque, Koskinen, and Zhang (2019).

socially responsible stakeholders (e.g., customers paying more for high-priced fair-trade products); but (3) firms can destroy value when they engage in "insider-initiated corporate philanthropy" (e.g., managers obtaining private benefits from using, for example, their favorite charities for making corporate contributions).

Other economists have taken this idea even further. Hart and Zingales (2017) asked, What is the most appropriate objective function of the firm? Shareholders should still keep decision rights because they are the "residual claimants" (i.e., they are paid only after all other claims are settled, and thus they bear the residual risk). The authors argued, however, that if shareholders are pro-social and if the profit-making activities and the damage-generating activities of firms are not separable, then firms should maximize shareholder welfare broadly and not simply maximize the market value of the firm. In the corporate charity example used by Friedman (1970) that I discussed earlier, $1 donated by the corporation is not worth more than $1 donated by shareholders. In many other cases, however, companies can take actions that shareholders cannot on their own. For example, Walmart's ability to restrict the sale of high-capacity assault rifles in its stores can be more effective in promoting desirable outcomes than if it instead takes the profits from those sales and returns them to shareholders, allowing shareholders to donate to gun control advocacy (or some other cause). Firms and asset managers should, therefore, expand their profit maximization objective to include pursuing policies that reflect their investors' desires. Doing so would still be in accord with the Friedman rule of shareholder primacy, but shareholders care about more than just financial results; they also have ethical and social concerns (perhaps the "ethical custom" in Friedman's quote).

A couple of contemporaneous working papers picked up this stream of literature in seeking to explore how investors might best interpret responsible investing based on ESG criteria from a theoretical perspective.[45] Pedersen, Fitzgibbons, and Pomorski (2019) suggested that ESG factors could be a reliable predictor of future returns if the factors contain relevant information about firm fundamentals or the preferences of responsible investors. Pastor, Stambaugh, and Taylor (2019) examined sustainable investing in equilibrium and found that ESG preferences move asset prices and stocks of "greener firms" by lowering *ex ante* CAPM alphas. However, these authors identified an "ESG risk factor" that captures investors' tastes for green holdings. If ESG

---

[45]Earlier theoretical work on the equilibrium effects of sustainable investing includes Heinkel, Kraus, and Zechner (2001). They explored how firms excluded by socially responsible investors suffer a reduction in risk sharing in their investor base and thus have a higher cost of capital, which affects their corporate behavior.

concerns strengthen, "green stocks" can outperform "brown stocks" over a period of time as the market transitions to this new set of ESG preferences, despite having lower alphas in the long run. They concluded that sustainable investing can lead to a positive social impact by inducing more investment by green firms and less investment by brown firms.

Does E&S/CSR Matter? The Evidence. A growing empirical literature examines whether companies that invest in CSR enhance their profitability and firm value, a relation often referred to as "doing well by doing good." The theoretical papers highlighted previously suggest that more-responsible companies deliver lower (not higher) returns to investors. That is to say, if a company is responsible and the market knows it is, the market price reflects this fact (by being higher than it otherwise would be), and so an investor pays for what she gets. Therefore, ESG-friendly companies benefit from a lower cost of capital (meaning a lower expected return on investor capital to undertake ESG-friendly projects), whereas "sin stocks" are "punished" with a higher cost of capital and thus investors' expectations of higher returns. In some ways, shareholders earning a lower expected return to "do good" is the way that ESG investing would generate an impact on real corporate investment choices: Companies are rewarded for their "good" behavior by facing lower capital costs. Alternatively, investors could still "do well by doing good" if either (1) companies with more-sustainable business models generate higher cash flows than the market expects or (2) investor preferences shift toward ESG-friendly companies over time for nonfinancial reasons and this shift is reflected in these firms experiencing higher returns in the transition years.

There have been several meta-analyses of CSR/ESG, but note that very few of the studies covered in those reviews have been published in what are generally considered to be among the top-ranked finance and economics academic journals. In a study commonly cited by PRI and others in the financial industry, Friede, Busch, and Bassen (2015) conducted a meta-analysis of 60 review studies that combined more than 2,200 unique primary studies. The authors documented that 90% of the academic studies found a nonnegative relationship between ESG and financial performance, of which 48% of vote-count studies and 63% of meta-analyses showed a positive correlation. This literature is unfortunately plagued by many issues: what aspect of CSR/ESG is being measured, the time horizon considered, what country is being examined, the data comparison methods, and so on. Also, what is the direction of causality? Is it more a case of "doing good by doing well" than of "doing well by doing good"? It could be that instead of ESG making firms more profitable, profitable firms may have the resources to invest in areas that positively influence ESG.

So is there evidence of "doing good but *not* well"? In a well-cited study, Hong and Kacperczyk (2009) found that "sin stocks" (tobacco, alcohol, and gambling firms) exhibit higher expected returns, lower analyst coverage, and less ownership from norm-constrained investors (such as pension funds).[46] These results are consistent with the existence of societal norms against funding "sin" activities. As mentioned previously, the intuition is that the reduction in demand resulting from investors being unwilling to hold companies with poor ESG exposures translates into lower stock prices today and higher returns in the future.[47] Masulis and Reza (2015) tested the Friedman (1970) view on corporate philanthropy. They used a quasi-experiment (based on the 2003 US dividend tax cut) and found that corporate giving is positively associated with CEO charity preferences but negatively associated with CEO shareholdings and corporate governance quality. These findings suggest that when corporate giving is in the interests of CEOs, they overinvest, which is not beneficial to shareholders.[48]

And what is the evidence for "doing good by doing well"? This outcome could be possible if investors consistently underestimate the benefits (or overestimate the costs) of being socially responsible. A good illustration of this situation is provided in the Edmans (2011) study on employee satisfaction and stock returns. The author found that the "100 Best Companies to Work For in America" outperformed their benchmarks. Stock markets seem to undervalue employee satisfaction even though such information is publicly available. The best companies' quarterly profits systematically beat analyst expectations. Employee satisfaction improves productivity, but the market seems not to take this dynamic into account.[49]

Recent studies have illustrated the view that the answer to the question of whether firms that "do good, do well" is "it depends," as with so many questions

---

[46]Similar evidence was found by Fabozzi, Ma, and Oliphant (2008). When revisiting the sin stock anomaly a decade later, however, Blitz and Fabozzi (2017) concluded that it can be explained by the two new quality factors (profitability and investment) in the more recently introduced Fama and French (2015) five-factor model. Dunn, Fitzgibbons, and Pomorski (2018) used Barra's risk model and found that firms with higher ESG ratings have lower risk.

[47]Statman and Glushkov (2009) concluded that as long as they do not shun sin stocks, investors can earn higher returns by tilting toward stocks with high social responsibility ratings.

[48]Cheng, Hong, and Shue (2013) reached similar conclusions.

[49]Edmans, Li, and Zhang (2017) expand internationally their study of employee satisfaction and stock returns. The "100 Best Companies to Work For" in 14 countries outperformed their peers in terms of long-run returns and future profitability in flexible markets (such as the United States and United Kingdom) but not in rigid labor markets (such as Germany).

in economics. The context matters, and here are a few dimensions. The first is that it might take some time for the market to learn. Borgers, Derwall, Koedijk, and Ter Horst (2013) found that high-CSR stocks outperformed low-CSR stocks during the period 1992–2004, but the authors failed to find significant results for 2004–2009. A second dimension involves how investors react to CSR news. Krüger (2015) found that investors have strong negative reactions to negative CSR news but, interestingly, weakly negative reactions to good CSR news (unless good news is offsetting a history of bad CSR news). Third, the outcome depends on how one measures CSR. Khan, Serafeim, and Yoon (2016) mapped CSR materiality guidance from the Sustainability Accounting Standards Board (SASB) to CSR scores and found that firms with high CSR materiality scores outperform firms with low materiality scores. Firms with good ratings on immaterial CSR issues do not significantly outperform firms with poor ratings on the same issues. A final example is that CSR companies might perform differently in good and bad times. Lins, Servaes, and Tamayo (2017) showed that firms with high CSR scores had higher stock returns than firms with low CSR scores during the 2008–09 financial crisis, providing some downside protection in volatile markets.

A final question is which firms are more likely to "do good"? Existing research points to several dimensions that drive companies to be more socially responsible. First, Liang and Renneboog (2017) took a global perspective and found that legal origins matter: Firms from common-law countries have lower CSR than civil-law firms, where a stakeholder perspective is more dominant. Management characteristics also seem to matter, such as management's political affiliation (Di Giuli and Kostovetsky 2014) or whether CEOs had daughters (Cronqvist and Yu 2017).

Do ESG/SRI Strategies Pay Off for Investors? Alongside the firm-level analysis on CSR, there is an active debate on the performance of funds focused on SRI/ESG investing. If ESG investing creates a binding constraint on portfolio optimization, then we should expect a performance cost. Naturally, ESG advocates and firms that offer sustainable financial products sometimes claim that ESG investing can enhance returns because of markets underpricing CSR information. In an early survey on the performance of SRI, Renneboog, Ter Horst, and Zhang (2008a) found little evidence that the average performance of SRI-focused funds in the United States and the United Kingdom differs significantly from that of conventional funds, noting that there is actually some degree of underpeformance in Europe and Asia Pacific. Most of those studies have small sample sizes, usually conducted in a single market and using limited time periods. In a companion paper,

Renneboog, Ter Horst, and Zhang (2008b) assembled a larger, global sample of SRI funds and concluded that SRI funds have negative alphas but their underperformance is not different from conventional funds. I will return to this issue to offer some new evidence later, because most of the growth in SRI has occurred in the decade since the Renneboog et al. (2008b) survey and ESG incorporation is not limited to the niche of specialized SRI funds but now encompasses more mainstream institutional investors.

Do Institutional Investors Influence E&S Outcomes? What is the role of institutional investors in implementing CSR/ESG in their portfolio companies? This is an area of active research. Similar to my review of the evidence for the role of different types of institutional investors in activism on G, investor heterogeneity is also likely to matter for E&S practices but not necessarily in the same ways.

The first investor dimension that could matter for E&S is investment horizon. Long-term investors should be more inclined toward ESG investing because ESG practices might have financial benefits only in the long term. Starks, Venkat, and Zhu (2018) examined this issue for US firms and found that institutions with longer horizons tend to invest more in firms with higher ESG scores and behave more patiently toward high-ESG firms. Similarly, Gibson and Krueger (2018) found that investors with longer investment horizons are associated with better portfolio-level ESG scores (better portfolio-level sustainability "footprints"). The authors found that investors with higher ESG portfolio footprints, especially with regard to environmental issues, have higher risk-adjusted returns.[50]

The investor's country of origin could matter as well. Dyck, Lins, Roth, and Wagner (2019) examined an international sample and found that firms with higher institutional ownership have better E&S scores. Interestingly, the effects are stronger with greater ownership by institutions from countries with stronger social and environmental norms (e.g., European investors as compared with US institutional investors) and that are PRI signatories. The authors used the Deepwater Horizon oil spill in 2010 as a quasi-experiment to help establish causality. Following the spill, firms in the oil extractive industry with greater institutional ownership improved their E&S policies more than firms with less institutional ownership did. While good G might be driven by US-based intuitions investing around the world, European investors may be "exporting" good E&S practices to firms in other regions.

---

[50]Glossner (2019) found that long-term institutions ensure, through monitoring, that managers do not blindly increase CSR but rather pursue a CSR strategy that reduces the risk of costly incidents.

Other recent work has examined the investor "ideology" of fund managers. Bolton, Li, Ravina, and Rosenthal (2019) examined proxy voting records to estimate institutional investor preferences and positioned institutions on a political spectrum from left to right. They found that, for instance, public pension funds and investors on the left support a more socially and environmentally friendly orientation of the firm. A second dimension pertains to what stand to take against management. Bubb and Catan (2019) also took a political approach to proxy voting.[51]

New Evidence on ESG Incorporation from the Principles for Responsible Investment

Highlights from this section:

- *European-based institutional investors lead the list of signatories of the PRI.*

- *When surveyed on ESG incorporation, a large fraction of PRI signatories report high levels of engagement, ESG integration, and negative screening.*

- *PRI signatory institutions "walk the ESG talk" in terms of their portfolio holdings, but US-domiciled signatories do so less than other signatories.*

- *PRI Collaboration Platform engagements improve the performance of target companies.*

To gain further insight into institutional investors' incorporation of ESG issues, I will now analyze some recent data from the Principles for Responsible Investment. Launched in 2006 by some of the world's largest institutional investors, with support from the United Nations (UN), the PRI aims to bring sustainability into capital markets, and at the end of 2019, it had more than 2,500 signatories around the world.[52] It is widely recognized as the

---

[51]For other studies on shareholder voting, see, for example, Flammer (2015), who compared the outcomes of E&S shareholder proposals that pass or fail by a small margin and found that successful CSR proposals lead to positive announcement returns and superior long-run financial performance. He, Kahraman, and Lowry (2019) showed that mutual fund support for E&S proposals has increased, but few such proposals pass—despite the fact that failed E&S proposals with higher investor support significantly predict future extreme negative stock returns and real events, such as negative E&S incidents.
[52]See www.unpri.org/about-the-pri.

most influential organization devoted to the advancement of ESG investing globally.[53] The PRI's six principles are as follows:

1. We will incorporate ESG issues into investment analysis and decision-making processes.

2. We will be active owners and incorporate ESG issues into our ownership policies and practices.

3. We will seek appropriate disclosure on ESG issues by the entities in which we invest.

4. We will promote acceptance and implementation of the Principles within the investment industry.

5. We will work together to enhance our effectiveness in implementing the Principles.

6. We will each report on our activities and progress toward implementing the Principles.

These principles can be signed by three organizational types: asset owners, investment managers, and service providers. "Asset owners" comprise pension funds, sovereign wealth funds, foundations, endowments, and insurance companies that could be concerned about ESG factors that affect the ability to meet their obligations to beneficiaries. "Investment managers" are investment fund companies and advisers with the ability to integrate ESG issues as they seek to maximize the value of their clients' investments. "Service providers" themselves do not manage assets and thus are excluded from the following analysis. By becoming signatories, PRI members commit to publicly reporting on their responsible investment considerations and decision making on a yearly basis (Principle 6).

How Do Institutional Investors Incorporate ESG Issues? A Look at the 2019 PRI Assessment Report. PRI signatories accounted for more than US$80 trillion of AUM in 2019.[54] **Figure 5** provides key data for the PRI Reporting Framework.[55] Panel A shows that European investors are the leaders in terms of number of signatories, but US and Canadian signatories control

---

[53]Greenwich Associates, "ESG Investing: The Global Phenomenon" (2018).

[54]Reporting takes place every year between January and March, and responses are interpreted to account for the previous calendar year (i.e., the 2019 report covers activities in 2018).

[55]Reported signatory data are publicly available via the PRI website, including access to transparency reports for each signatory. The PRI shares data with academics and think tanks for noncommercial purposes upon signing the relevant terms and conditions. See www.unpri.org/signatories/how-to-access-reported-data.

Figure 5.   Statistics on PRI Signatories Reporting in 2019: AUM and Number of Signatories

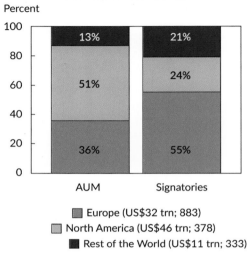

A. Breakdown by Region

Europe (US$32 trn; 883)

North America (US$46 trn; 378)

Rest of the World (US$11 trn; 333)

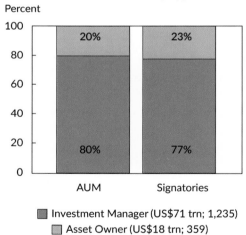

B. Breakdown by Type

Investment Manager (US$71 trn; 1,235)

Asset Owner (US$18 trn; 359)

(continued)

Figure 5.   Statistics on PRI Signatories Reporting in 2019: AUM and Number of Signatories *(continued)*

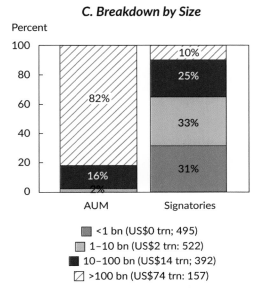

C. Breakdown by Size

- ■ <1 bn (US$0 trn; 495)
- □ 1–10 bn (US$2 trn: 522)
- ■ 10–100 bn (US$14 trn; 392)
- ▨ >100 bn (US$74 trn: 157)

D. Percentage AUM by Asset Class

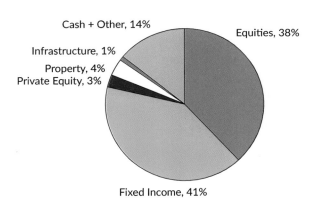

Cash + Other, 14%

Infrastructure, 1%

Property, 4%

Private Equity, 3%

Equities, 38%

Fixed Income, 41%

more of the assets under management. Panel B presents the breakdown in terms of asset owners (who manage their capital directly) versus investment managers (who manage on behalf of their clients).[56] Panel C shows that most large institutional investors are now signatories, which might reflect that

---

[56]The analysis ignores service providers (e.g., ESG rating or consulting firms) because these do not directly have assets under management.

37

Table 2. Top PRI Reporting Signatories by Region (as of 2019)

Region	Investor Name	Signatory Year	Type*	Total AUM (in US$ bn)
Europe	Amundi	2006	IM	$1,626
	AXA Group	2012	AO	1,625
	Credit Suisse Group AG	2014	IM	1,354
	Legal & General Inv. Mgmt.	2010	IM	1,201
	Norges Bank Investment Management	2006	AO	976
North America	BlackRock	2008	IM	5,976
	The Vanguard Group, Inc.	2014	IM	4,867
	State Street Global Advisors	2012	IM	2,511
	Fidelity Investments	2017	IM	2,420
	Capital Group	2010	IM	1,677
Rest of the world	GPIF	2015	AO	1,377
	Japan Post Insurance Co.	2017	AO	660
	Korea National Pension Service	2009	AO	569
	Sumitomo Mitsui Trust Asset Mgmt.	2006	IM	554
	Nippon Life Insurance Co.	2017	AO	529

*IM stands for investment manager; AO stands for asset owner.

PRI membership is now an important requirement for investment managers in order to obtain investment mandates from clients. Panel D provides the reported AUM distribution by asset class. The large majority of PRI signatory assets are in equities and fixed income, so the remainder of the statistics will concentrate on these asset classes.[57]

Table 2 shows that the top PRI signatories are some of the world's largest institutional investors in Europe, North America, and the rest of the world.

Although there is no official taxonomy, **Table 3** summarizes the different types of responsible investing strategies in the PRI Reporting Framework, which follows those developed by CFA Institute (2015) and used by the Global Sustainable Investment Alliance (2019), among others. These same strategies were highlighted by Amel-Zadeh and Serafeim (2018) in their survey on why and how institutional investors use ESG information.

---

[57]The PRI Reporting Framework also includes other asset classes (private equity, property, infrastructure, hedge funds, and inclusive finance), which are not covered in the following analysis.

Table 3. Types of Responsible Investing Strategies

Buy? |————————————————————————————————————→ Sell?

Screening:	Integration:	Engagement:
• **Negative screening:** The exclusion from a portfolio of certain sectors, companies, or practices based on specific ESG criteria.	The systematic and explicit inclusion of ESG factors into financial analysis.	• **Individual:** The investor's internal staff using shareholder power to influence corporate behavior, including through direct corporate engagement (i.e., communicating with senior management and company boards) and filing shareholder proposals.
• **Positive/best-in-class screening:** Investment in companies selected for positive ESG performance relative to industry peers.		
• **Norm-based screening:** Screening of investments against minimum standards of business practice based on international norms.		• **Collaborative:** The conduct of corporate engagement, as defined above; however, it is undertaken jointly with other investors.
Thematic: Investment in assets specifically related to sustainability (e.g., clean energy, green technology, or sustainable agriculture).		• **Internal voting:** The use of proxy voting guided by ESG guidelines where the voting decisions are undertaken internally and not outsourced to an external service provider.

The first type of strategies concerns decisions on identifying companies in which to invest. The most longstanding strategy is negative screening, which—based on moral, norm-based, or ethical considerations—excludes stocks with worse ESG characteristics from a portfolio (Hong and Kacperczyk 2009). For example, these include exclusions based on geography (e.g., companies from South Africa in the 1970s under apartheid) or certain industries or activities (e.g., tobacco, owing to the health impact of the companies' products) for ethical reasons or to avoid reputational damage. Filtering the investment universe to exclude companies with controversial practices or events offers perhaps the most direct way to address ESG goals. Instead of avoiding companies with exposures to certain ESG risks, another approach is to align capital with desirable sustainable outcomes. Doing so leads to the use of methods of positive screening (investing in best-in-class ESG companies) or norm-based screening (e.g., using the UN Global Compact Principles). Thematic investing consists of dedicated investment vehicles that allocate capital directly to sectors that are positioned to take advantage of certain ESG themes (e.g., renewable energy), and in fixed income, these include green bonds (which finance environmental projects) and social bonds (for social projects).

The second type of strategies consists of engagement with corporate management and occurs subsequent to making an investment. As mentioned previously, negative screening could limit an investor's impact on driving ESG change because without holding shares of a company, an investor cannot vote. In contrast, through engagement (also known as active ownership or stewardship), investors can use their position as partial owners of companies to improve how those companies are managing or disclosing ESG performance. Engagement involves discussing ESG issues with management (via private meetings or letters and dialogue during earnings calls or roadshows) or formally expressing approval or disapproval through the votes that their shareholdings entitle them to. Investors can engage individually, in collaboration with other investors, or through an outsourced engagement service provider.

A third (and perhaps more comprehensive) strategy is integration, which consists of changing traditional investment processes to incorporate ESG data and insights into the overall evaluation of an investment. In this approach, investment teams use sustainability data to create a more holistic view of investment risks and opportunities, regardless of whether the investment fund has a sustainable mandate. It includes the ESG information during the research phase, security valuation, or portfolio construction—or later, during monitoring and risk management.

Let us now turn to the data reported to the PRI.[58] **Figure 6** shows the frequency with which PRI signatories report the use of responsible investment strategies (what economists call the "extensive margin"). These strategies are not mutually exclusive, with most signatories using multiple strategies that can overlap with one another. In terms of their holdings of listed equities, the dominant strategies pursued by PRI signatories are engagement, ESG integration, and negative screening. Thematic strategies are still a niche market. These patterns also hold for fixed-income investments, for which the most

---

[58]I examined exclusively ESG incorporation in active equity and fixed-income strategies (the Direct Listed Equities Incorporation, Direct Listed Equity Active Ownership, and Direct Fixed Income modules). I did not examine passive strategies, but these can also take ESG issues into account. For indexed investing, the incorporation of ESG occurs typically in constructing investable indexes designed for sustainable investors to track and benchmark their performance. ESG indexes are still relatively young and have been created on the basis of ESG ratings that are typically a subset of the constituents or a different weighing compared with broad market indexes. The indexes are built on the basis of backtested data, and some of them try to limit tracking error compared with the broad market indexes with improvement in ESG scores. For a case study, see P. Matos, M. M. Frank, and A. Fernstrom, "Just Capital," Darden Case No. UVA-F-1844 (17 August 2019). Available at https://papers.ssrn.com/sol3/papers.cfm?abstract_id=3331358.

popular strategies are also screening (to potentially limit downside risk) and ESG integration.[59]

In terms of the amount of AUM invested in each approach (**Figure 7** and **Figure 8**, the intensive margin), signatories report that more than three-quarters of the AUM are covered by integration strategies, followed by screening strategies (about half of AUM). Thematic strategies are still niche (only a little over one-tenth of AUM). There is significant heterogeneity in terms of how the adoption of certain strategies differs across regions, investor types, and investor size. PRI signatories from Europe and asset owners have a higher use of screening.

Figure 6. ESG Incorporation—Extensive Margin: Percentage of PRI Signatories Using a Given Approach

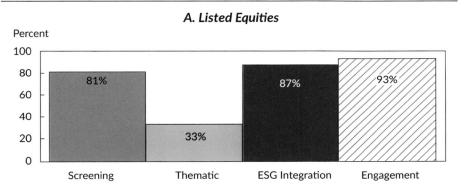

A. Listed Equities

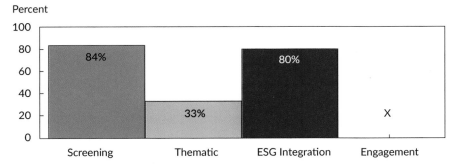

B. Fixed Income

(continued)

---

[59]Because bondholders are not company owners, engagement is not a reported strategy for fixed income.

Figure 6. ESG Incorporation—Extensive Margin: Percentage of PRI Signatories Using a Given Approach *(continued)*

C. Listed Equities, Breakdown

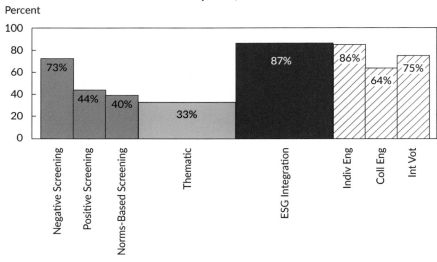

D. Fixed Income, Breakdown

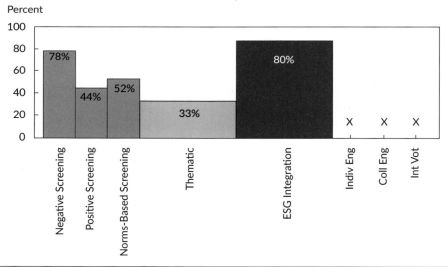

Notes: This figure is computed by the author based on the responses in the PRI report to the Direct Listed Equities Incorporation (Question LEI 04.1), Direct Listed Equity Active Ownership (LEA 02.1 and LEA 12.1), and Direct Fixed Income modules (FI 04.1; in this case, an equal-weighted average of the percentage in all types of debt is taken—sovereign, financials, corporate, and securitized).

Divestment is typically seen as a last resort. Some studies point to the considerable financial costs—for example, in fossil fuel divestment (Bessembinder 2016)—but some large institutional investors are nonetheless divesting what are viewed as unsustainable assets.[60] For example, NBIM, the organization

Figure 7.   ESG Incorporation—Intensive Margin: Percentage of Listed Equity Portfolio AUM to Which Approach Is Applied

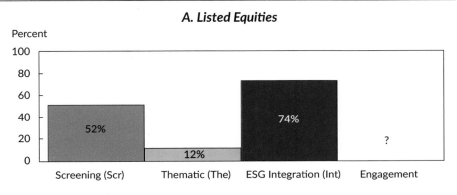

A. *Listed Equities*

B. *By Region*

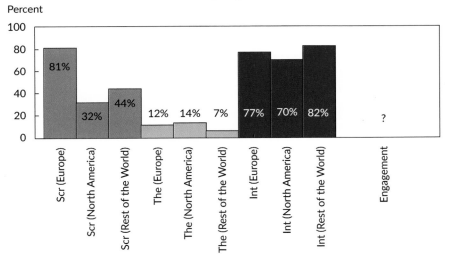

(continued)

---

[60]Arabella Investments, "The Global Fossil Fuel Divestment and Clean Energy Investment Movement: 2018 Report" (2019). For a case study, see Chambers, Dimson, and Quigley (2019).

Figure 7.   ESG Incorporation—Intensive Margin: Percentage of Listed Equity Portfolio AUM to Which Approach Is Applied *(continued)*

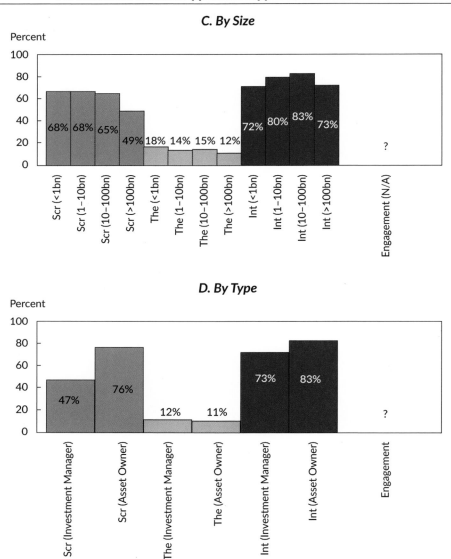

Note: This figure is computed by the author based on the responses in the PRI report to the Direct Listed Equities Incorporation module (Question LEI 01.1).

responsible for managing Norway's sovereign wealth fund, decided to divest from coal and, more recently, a range of oil and gas companies.[61] Others argue that if some institutional investors sell their shares, there will be willing buyers, thus diminishing the voice and impact of responsible institutional investors.[62]

Figure 8. ESG Incorporation—Intensive Margin: Percentage of Listed Fixed-Income Portfolio AUM to Which Approach Is Applied

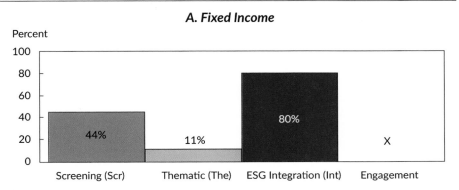

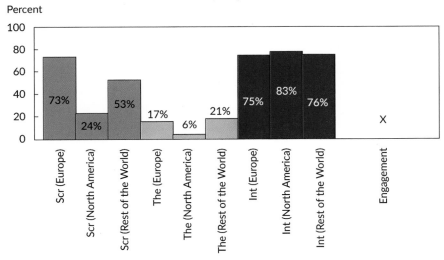

(continued)

[61] See Atta-Darkua (2019).
[62] Andrew Edgecliffe-Johnson and Billy Nauman, "Fossil Fuel Divestment Has 'Zero' Climate Impact, Says Bill Gates," *Financial Times* (17 September 2019).

45

Figure 8. ESG Incorporation—Intensive Margin: Percentage of Listed Fixed-Income Portfolio AUM to Which Approach Is Applied *(continued)*

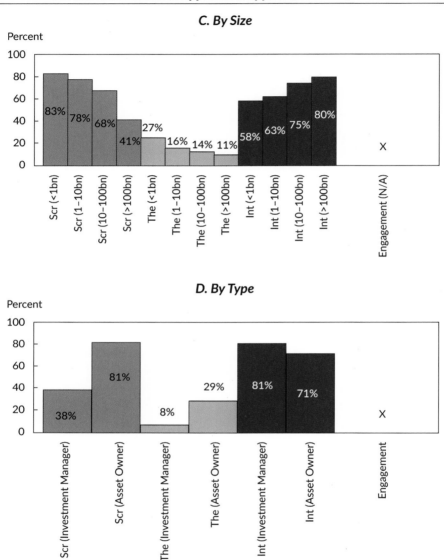

Notes: This figure is computed by the author based on the responses in the PRI report to the Direct Fixed Income module (Question FI 01.1). A value-weighted average of the percentage in all types of debt is taken—sovereign, financials, corporates, and securitized.

Highlights from Study 1: Gibson, Glossner, Krueger, Matos, and Steffen (2019). In a recent working paper, my co-authors and I combined the PRI Reporting Framework data described previously with institutional investor equity portfolio holdings data obtained from FactSet Ownership (which was featured prominently earlier in this review and was used in prior studies on institutional ownership). In Gibson, Glossner, Krueger, Matos, and Steffen (GGKMS 2019), we documented the considerable growth in the number and equity AUM of PRI signatory institutions since 2006, with more than $1 of every $2 of institutionally managed equities by the end of the sample period (2017). We found considerable investor heterogeneity, with larger and European-based investors more likely to commit to responsible investing versus other global regions.

To test whether PRI signatory institutions "walk the ESG talk," GGKMS (2019) further augmented these data with stock-level ESG scores from three rating providers (Thomson Reuters ASSET4, MSCI IVA, and Sustainalytics) and calculated each institutional investor's "ESG footprint" (the value-weighted average standardized ESG scores for its stock portfolio, as in Gibson and Krueger 2018). We found that institutional investors who join the PRI exhibit better portfolio-level ESG performance, but the differences are not overwhelmingly large. **Figure 9** shows that although these positive differences in ESG scores hold for non-US investors, for

Figure 9. ESG Portfolio Footprints of PRI vs. Non-PRI Signatories: Difference in Portfolio ESG Scores between PRI and Non-PRI Signatories— Multivariate Regressions

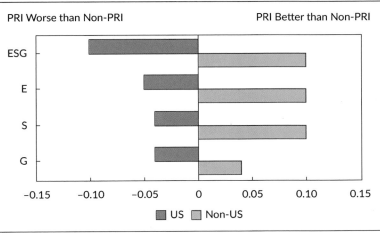

Note: Results are subject to updates; please refer to the source.
Source: GGKMS (2019).

US-domiciled investors, there is actually a negative (but not statistically significant) difference between PRI signatories and other institutions. This finding could be the result of differing interpretations of fiduciary duties in the United States—for example, the DOL guidance for retirement plans stresses that fiduciaries must not put ESG goals ahead of financial ones, as discussed earlier.

Next, we explored the ESG implementation strategies in greater detail using the PRI Reporting Framework data described previously. When we estimated the performance impact across each responsible investment strategy, however, we found no strong evidence for added performance for any of the ESG implementation strategies described in Panels A and C of Figure 6 and Panels A–D of Figure 7.

Finally, we analyzed the benefits and costs associated with responsible investing. As discussed previously, an active debate exists as to whether ESG investing is an effective approach to enhance expected returns. GGKMS (2019) uncovered some evidence that PRI signatories appear to have lower portfolio returns on their respective equity strategies versus non-PRI signatories. When we analyzed PRI signatory strategies, we did find evidence that some ESG strategies lower portfolio risk.[63] We conclude that responsible investing has acted as a risk management tool rather than as a return enhancer.

Highlights from Study 2: Dimson, Karakas, and Li (2019). A recent working paper by Dimson et al. (2019) examined in detail one of the ESG substrategies: coordinated engagements (one of the forms of engagement in Panel C of Figure 6). In seeking to enhance their collective influence on ESG issues, PRI signatories can pool engagement resources through the PRI Collaboration Platform. This pooling approach may help alleviate the free-rider problem recognized as a primary deterrent of active ownership.

Dimson et al. (2019) studied 31 PRI-coordinated engagement projects initiated between 2007 and 2015. They defined engagement as a sequence of interactions between an investor and a company on a specific issue; examples include carbon disclosure, anti-corruption measures and transparency, and ensuring that supply chains do not involve conflict areas. The study sample included a total of 1,671 engagement sequences targeting 964 unique publicly listed firms located in 63 countries by 224 unique investment organizations from 24 countries. Success was defined by PRI professionals on the basis of a set of criteria and scorecards defined at the beginning of each project.

---

[63]Dunn et al. (2018) found that firms with higher ESG ratings have lower risk.

Dimson et al. (2019) documented that successful coordinated engagements result in improved financial performance of the target companies, improved shareholder returns, and strengthened relationships between investors and companies. The authors found that success rates are higher when there is a lead investor who is based in the same country as the targeted firm and is larger in terms of AUM and investment stake. Support by major institutional investors also plays a positive role. Successful collaborative engagements are beneficial for shareholders exhibiting positive abnormal stock returns for the three years following engagement. Evidence also points to lower risk (as measured by lower variability of returns) and increased post-engagement accounting performance.

This study builds on an earlier study on ESG engagements in the United States by Dimson, Karakas, and Li (2015) that examined more than 2,000 private engagements with US public companies by one large institutional investor. Collaboration among activists played an instrumental role in increasing the success rate of the engagements. Hoepner, Oikonomou, Sautner, Starks, and Zhou (2019) examined similar data and showed that ESG engagements also reduce downside risk.

Many Open Questions

Highlights from this section:

- *Research highlights the many data quality issues and the ESG rating dispersion among data providers.*

- *There are concerns over the growing influence of proxy advisory firms.*

- *Asset classes beyond public equities are underresearched.*

- *There is very limited research on how ESG investing affects real outcomes, how much clients are willing to sacrifice in returns, and "impact investing."*

ESG Ratings and Data Quality Issues? ESG data have become the backbone of responsible investing, with an aim to capture information otherwise unavailable from standard financial statements but deemed material from an ESG perspective. Although independent ESG data providers originally served a small client base of institutional investors, in response to investor demand and growing availability, such data are now more widely available, including in such financial terminals as Bloomberg and at various websites.[64] The data serve to provide a useful snapshot of a company's performance on a range of ESG issues.[65]

The rapid growth in the availability of ESG data does, however, raise concerns about the quality of the data. Originally, ESG data were typically sourced from scattered company financial reports, but an increasing number of public companies are now publishing annual sustainability reports.[66] This increase is a result, in part, of companies being increasingly required by securities regulators or stock exchanges to integrate sustainability information into their reporting cycles. The metrics and indicators from these disclosures, however, have biases, may be subject to "greenwashing" (Yang 2019), are difficult to compare, and are often inconsistent across firms.[67] There are also serious challenges in obtaining coverage related to ESG issues for smaller companies and for certain regions (e.g., coverage is less available for emerging markets). Furthermore, missing data present a meaningful problem for conducting reliable historical analysis. ESG data providers further obtain data from publicly available resources, such as regulatory or government documents, NGOs, and print media. This has evolved to include alternative information found on the internet (e.g., employee satisfaction ratings on Glassdoor.com). The concern here is that these approaches might flag only extreme events and could be influenced by social perception rather than more objective metrics.

---

[64]For example, the ESG coverage for MSCI ACWI companies by MSCI (one of the ESG data providers) has increased from 34% in 2009 to 58% in 2017 (BlackRock, "Sustainability: The Future of Investing" [February 2019]). Smaller-capitalization companies with a lower investor base still have lower coverage.

[65]For a quick overview of ESG data providers, their methodologies, and usage, see "ESG Reports and Ratings: What They Are, Why They Matter," Harvard Law School Forum on Corporate Governance and Financial Regulation (27 July 2017).

[66]In 2017, 85% of S&P 500 Index companies published sustainability reports, up from 11% in 2011 (Governance & Accountability Institute, "Flash Report: 60% of Russell 1000® Are Publishing Sustainability Reports, G&A Institute's 2018 Inaugural Benchmark Study Shows" [2018]).

[67]For example, the EU mandated the disclosure of nonfinancial and diversity information through Directive 2014/95/EU. The UN's Sustainable Stock Exchanges (SSE) Initiative has also worked with stock exchanges to promote improved ESG reporting instruments. The number of sustainability reporting instruments around the world has grown, with around two-thirds of these identified as mandatory (KPMG International, GRI, United Nations Environment Programme, and Centre for Corporate Governance in Africa, "Carrots & Sticks: Global Trends in Sustainability Reporting Regulation and Policy" [2016]). There have been some standardization efforts, such as the Sustainability Accounting Standards Board, the Global Reporting Initiative, and the Task Force on Climate-Related Financial Disclosures, but none of these reporting schemes is universally accepted.

ESG scores are clearly becoming more important, but a second concern relates to the considerable divergence in the metrics and methodologies used among ESG data providers. ESG scores seek to provide a quantitative measure regarding a firm's ESG performance and guides investors in comparing and ranking companies relative to industry peers. The scores can be included in valuation models, aggregated at the portfolio level (as in GGKMS 2019), and used for screening, benchmarking, or to build investment products. The more commonly used ESG scores are collected *ex ante* or consist of conduct-based ratings (Krueger 2019), which attempt to capture how exposed a company might be to an ESG issue and its ability to manage that exposure.[68] This means an ESG score is an amalgamation of indicators (e.g., CO_2-equivalent emissions, labor issues, and board diversity).

There is no exhaustive list of agreed-upon ESG issues, however, and even if there were, the metrics used are naturally hard to combine in a useful quantitative way. Although some criteria, such as carbon emissions, can be objectively measured, many ESG factors require subjective decisions, such as a tick-the-box approach from assessors. For example, the environmental harm of certain energy sources can be reasonably disputed. Consider how even the environmental impact of electrical vehicles depends on how one weights the inputs (energy and rare earth minerals) used in producing and operating the vehicle versus its outputs (zero emissions from the cars).[69] Similarly, the social factors may depend on social norms. Governance factors can also be debated (e.g., whether a particular type of governing board known as a classified board should be considered value enhancing or value destroying is widely debated in academia). ESG ratings vary in terms of the number of ESG indicators and how each factor is weighted in generating an overall ESG score. The scale of the ESG ratings also varies according to data provider.

Practitioners have further pointed to potential biases in ESG ratings: (1) size (larger companies may receive better ESG reviews because they can dedicate greater resources to prepare and publish ESG disclosures and control reputational risk); (2) geography (higher ESG assessments for companies domiciled in regions with greater reporting requirements); and (3) industry bias (normalizing ESG ratings by industry can oversimplify them). A final issue is that ESG ratings may be backward looking and thus may fail to

---

[68]There are also other ratings that are *ex post* incidence based or opportunity product based. See Krueger (2019).

[69]James Mackintosh, "Is Tesla or Exxon More Sustainable? It Depends Whom You Ask," *Wall Street Journal* (17 September 2018). As an example, this article described how Tesla, ranked by MSCI at the top of the industry, was ranked as the worst car manufacturer globally on ESG issues by FTSE, whereas Sustainalytics put it in the middle.

capture how a company may be making an honest effort to improve its sustainability record. A "controversial stock" today might not be a "controversial stock" tomorrow; for example, incumbent energy firms may be fossil fuel intensive but best positioned to explore alternative energy sources in the future.

Complicating matters, as shown by Gibson, Krueger, Riand, and Schmidt (2019), ESG ratings diverge considerably. They drew this conclusion using ESG scores from six prominent data providers (Thomson Reuters, MSCI, Sustainalytics, KLD, Bloomberg, and Inrate) for S&P 500 firms from 2013 to 2017. To ensure comparability of ESG ratings across providers, the authors rank-normalized ESG scores between 0 and 1 in each month by firm. The authors found that the average correlation between overall ESG ratings of the six providers was less than 50%.[70] Surprisingly, the average correlation was highest for the environmental dimension and lowest for governance factors.

Chatterji, Durand, Levine, and Touboul (2016) attributed the observed disagreement in ESG ratings to a lack of a shared view of what it means for a firm to be socially responsible and also the lack of agreement on metrics to use to measure it. Gibson, Krueger, Riand, and Schmidt (2019) focused on the legal origin of ESG rating firms and found that civil-law-based ESG data providers have stronger views regarding labor issues and social protection, whereas common-law ESG data providers emphasize investor protection and stronger protection of shareholders rights, as well as a stronger view on other governance issues. The authors showed that disagreement is reduced when data vendors are stratified according to legal origin. Kotsantonis and Serafeim (2019) pointed to inconsistencies in terms of how issuing companies report data, how peer groups are defined, and ESG data imputation.

Berg, Koelbel, and Rigobon (2019) decomposed ESG rating discrepancy into scope, measurement, and weights. The authors concluded that measurement divergence explains more than 50% of the overall divergence and detected a rater effect (the measurement is influenced by a rating agency's view of the analyzed company).

All these reasons underscore the potential hazards of simply relying on a final ESG score for investment decisions. In assessing ESG risks and opportunities, investors should thus make an independent assessment based on their own due diligence efforts (but, of course, resources are limited in many investment organizations in terms of staff or data budgets). There are also concerns that ESG ratings may at some point rise in stature and achieve a

---

[70]This number is lower than typically observed for credit ratings from Moody's and Standard & Poor's, which typically have a 90% or higher correlation (Berg, Koelbel, and Rigobon 2019).

similar influence as credit ratings. Because many investors rely on credit rating agencies to determine which assets to invest in (with some distortionary effects as shown during the global financial crisis), ESG ratings could also in the future become sufficiently influential on investors' allocations.

An Overreliance on Proxy Advisory Firms? The two most predominant proxy advisory firms, ISS and Glass Lewis, play an important role in the institutional investment ecosystem by advising institutional investors on voting in corporate elections and advocating better corporate governance. Several academic studies have reported on the influence of these two proxy firms. Cai, Garner, and Walkling (2009) analyzed director elections and concluded that ISS has a strong impact on voting, especially when it recommends that shareholders vote against an individual director. Alexander, Chen, Seppi, and Spatt (2010) documented that ISS recommendations in corporate proxy contests are predictive about contest outcomes and informative about the ability of dissidents to add value. Malenko and Shen (2016) found that a negative ISS recommendation results in a 25% reduction in positive votes. Larcker, McCall, and Ormazabal (2015) raised concerns about "outsourcing" shareholder voting. Despite their influence, it is worth noting that proxy advisers have limited resources with skeletal staff in relation to the number of companies for which they are making recommendations.

The influence of proxy advisers has led the SEC to propose new proxy rules. The rules would impose new requirements on shareholder advisers to provide companies with advance copies of their advice before it goes out to investors.[71] ISS filed a lawsuit against the SEC in response, and there were extensive lobby efforts by both institutional investors and corporate management.[72] This issue provides an area ripe for more extensive academic research in the coming years.

Going beyond Equities: Other Asset Classes? I mentioned at the outset that the focus of this survey was ESG incorporation in public equities (where more academic research has been conducted), but it is important to highlight some of the first academic work on other asset classes. ESG incorporation in debt markets may have greater potential because withholding new debt financing or refusing to refinance is likely to have more influence on firms' operations and ESG choices than an investor buying or selling secondary market shares. Previously, I showed some PRI data on ESG incorporation

---

[71]Kadhim Shubber, "US SEC Moves Forward with Tougher Proxy Rule Proposals," *Financial Times* (5 November 2019).

[72]Attracta Mooney and Patrick Temple-West, "Battle Royale: SEC Locks Horns with Investors over Proxy Advisers," *Financial Times* (9 December 2019).

in fixed income. Chava (2014) and Hoepner, Oikonomou, Scholtens, and Schröder (2016) found that firms with high environmental and social concerns face higher interest rates on bank loans. Another emerging literature focuses on labeled bonds (primarily green bonds, whose proceeds are invested in projects that generate environmental benefits).[73] Flammer (2019) studied the "green bond boom" in recent years and found a significant increase in environmental performance after the announcement of corporate green bond issues that are independently certified. Zerbib (2019) uncovered a small yield differential, suggesting that investments with positive ESG scores can be expected to earn somewhat lower returns. Regarding US municipal bonds, Baker, Bergstresser, Serafeim, and Wurgler (2018) found that green bonds tend to be priced at a small premium, but Larcker and Watts (2019), however, failed to find such a "greenium" when matching a sample green security to nearly identical nongreen municipal securities.

In terms of other asset classes, another interesting case is real estate, where REITs may have portfolio exposure to properties that are environmentally certified. Eichholtz, Kok, and Quigley (2010, 2013) studied the valuation and returns of green buildings. Eichholtz, Kok, and Yonder (2012) concluded that there is no significant relation between the greenness of REITs' property portfolios and abnormal stock returns. These and other asset classes, such as infrastructure finance, private equity, and hedge funds, are still underresearched.

What Is Driving Investor Flows, and How Much Are Investors Willing to Sacrifice in Returns to Promote ESG? What is driving institutional investors to incorporate E&S considerations? Recent studies have examined the role of client (end-investor) demand. Hartzmark and Sussman (2019) examined the introduction of the Morningstar mutual fund sustainability "globe" ratings in 2016 to show that investors value sustainability criteria. After the introduction of Morningstar ESG ratings, US funds with low ESG ratings subsequently observed net outflows while funds with high ESG ratings had net inflows. In a related study, Ceccarelli, Ramelli, and Wagner (2019) examined the mutual fund investor inflows to the recently introduced eco-labeling of "low carbon designation" funds by Morningstar in the United States and Europe. The authors found that fund managers tend to adjust their

---

[73]Fender, McMorrow, Sahakyan, and Zulaica (2019) estimated that green bonds have grown from less than $50 billion in 2014 to close to $230 billion in 2018. There are some green bond standards (e.g., Certification Scheme of the Climate Bonds Initiative) helping safeguard investors against greenwashing, but the European Commission is currently working on clearer definitions surrounding the asset class. There are also some discussion plans to lower capital requirements for banks on green investments.

holdings toward climate-friendlier stocks in order to keep investors. Other studies have provided unique investor-level evidence. Riedl and Smeets (2017) used administrative and survey data to study what influences individual investors to hold socially responsible mutual funds. The authors found that social preferences play a role but financial motives are less important in driving individual investors' SRI mutual fund choices. Bauer, Ruof, and Smeets (2020) conducted a field experiment with beneficiaries of a Dutch pension fund to study to what degree individual beneficiaries within the pension system prefer their pension savings to be used to promote sustainability. The authors found that 68% of the participants favored an approach that invests their pension savings in a sustainable manner (even if it implied lower returns). The willingness to pay, however, is very much an open area for research.

Going beyond ESG Metrics: How to Measure Real Effects? There are several concerns as to whether ESG investing and CSR by firms lead to real corporate change. ESG incorporation could simply constitute a box-ticking exercise, leading to little in the way of real outcomes on the desired ESG goals. This scenario could be the case if ESG investing is left to specialists within money management companies and does not affect portfolio decisions. Companies themselves may also only cosmetically adjust their ESG measures, without changing any of their investment and operating decisions.

The question ultimately is whether ESG investing is truly helping to achieve societal goals. Beyond climate change, the UN-defined Sustainable Development Goals (SDGs) are a set of 17 economic, social, and environmental goals that will work together to make the world more sustainable by 2030.[74] They include a mix of ESG issues, such as the eradication of poverty (Goal 1), gender equality (Goal 5), and climate action (Goal 13), that all require the mobilization of private capital. Schramade (2017) listed some of the potential investment opportunities, but not all SDGs are equally investable, and reporting on SDGs is unfortunately too scarce to produce effective outcomes. Serafeim (2018) discussed some of the SDGs, but I am aware of almost no academic research in top-ranked finance journals on how ESG investing is contributing to the achievement of the SDGs.

Bauer et al. (2020) found in their field experiment, however, that a majority of pension plan participants support increased investment based on the SDGs. Although investment managers today typically elicit clients' risk preferences, most ignore social preferences as part of their assessment. Looking ahead, however, this concern could be alleviated, at least for European-based investors, because the European Commission intends in the near future to

---

[74]See www.undp.org/content/undp/en/home/sustainable-development-goals.html.

introduce a formal requirement that "investment firms [should ask retail investors] about their preferences for sustainable investments."[75]

Impact Investing: Investing or Philanthropy? One area that I did not cover in this survey (because it lies outside public capital markets) relates to "impact investing," a topic that has received considerable attention in recent years. The main idea behind impact investing is to use the tools of entrepreneurial finance to support social enterprises. There is no agreed-upon definition, however, and the concept can span many activities, such as microfinance, affordable housing, water and sanitation, and health care. It can also be deployed by a range of asset managers, from venture capital and development finance institutions to family offices or foundations that use impact investments alongside traditional grant making to achieve their program goals. Cole, Gandhi, and Brumme (2018) offered some background. Impact investing is increasing in popularity. The Global Impact Investing Network (2019) estimated that impact investing organizations manage more than US$500 billion, exceeding the US$428 billion that Giving USA (2019) estimated that American individuals, bequests, foundations, and corporations gave in philanthropy.

Barber, Morse, and Yasuda (2019) examined "impact funds"—private equity funds that have a dual objective of generating both financial and social returns. They found that venture capital funds that aim not only for financial return but also for social impact earn lower returns than traditional funds earn. The authors argued that investors derive nonpecuniary utility from investing in dual-objective funds. Interestingly, tests that segment by region showed that LP investors from Europe dominate the demand for impact funds. Geczy, Jeffers, Musto, and Tucker (2019) conducted an in-depth study of contracts for impact investing funds. Others, such as Chowdhry, Davies, and Waters (2019) and Oehmke and Opp (2019), have explored the theoretical underpinnings, but the topic area still remains underresearched.

Conclusion

Over the course of this survey, I traced the evolution of the growing body of research on ESG investing, starting with corporate governance and the increasing role played by institutional investors in public markets worldwide. I documented some effects of institutional shareholder activism in the United States and the role of foreign institutions in making non-US markets converge toward US governance standards. An open debate remains, however, about what comes next as investors increasingly pursue index-based strategies,

---

[75]See ec.europa.eu/info/sites/info/files/180524-sustainable-finance-factsheet_en.pdf.

in turn leading to a growing concentration of indexed assets among the "Big Three" index managers. On the environmental and social dimension, the biggest focus is on climate change, and here European-based investors and regulators are leading the way in addressing this pressing challenge. I presented some new evidence from PRI signatory institutions, but any research conclusions are still preliminary in answering the questions of to what degree institutions really "walk the (green) talk" and what are the ultimate effects on the behavior of portfolio companies.

Although the last section covered some open questions for research, I have undoubtedly omitted many other pressing ESG issues. In the environmental dimension, one such example is that much research is still needed on the role of central banks in promoting a sustainable financial system. A recent report by Bolton, Despres, Pereira da Silva, Samama, and Svartzman (2020) warned of the potential "green swan" risk resulting from climate change with potentially large financially disruptive consequences. In terms of social concerns, there is still little research focus on ways of tapping sustainable finance to address the rising societal problems associated with wealth inequality. Hopefully, these and other areas can be more fully addressed in future research efforts.

Readers might walk away with a sense that research to date on the impact of ESG investing has been quite skeptical. I prefer to characterize the current state of the literature as having a "healthy dose of skepticism," but as mentioned previously, much more remains to be explored. Here, I leave the reader with a call to action. For the industry practitioner, I believe that the investment industry should strive to achieve positive societal goals. CFA Institute provides an exemplary case in its Future of Finance series (www. cfainstitute.org/research/future-finance), making the case that in order to meet client expectations in the years ahead, firms must necessarily commit additional resources to considering ESG issues (CFA Institute 2018). For the academic community, I suggest we ramp up research aimed at tackling some of the pressing societal goals. As Zingales (2015) pointed out in his American Finance Association presidential address "Does Finance Benefit Society?," a disconnect exists between academics' and society's perceptions of the value of finance, particularly in the years following the global financial crisis. I want the reader to come away from reading this survey with a sense of optimism that practitioners and academics can and will work together to identify meaningful ways to better harness the power of global financial markets to address the pressing ESG issues facing our society today and in the years to come.

I thank Miguel Ferreira, Rajna Gibson, Philipp Krueger, Simon Glossner, and Tom Steffen, as well as Mikael Homanen, Justin Hopkins, and especially Rodney Sullivan, CFA, for detailed feedback. Simon Glossner provided excellent research assistance. This research was possible through the support of the Richard A. Mayo Center for Asset Management at the University of Virginia Darden School of Business.

Bibliography

Admati, A.R. 2017. "A Skeptical View of Financialized Corporate Governance." *Journal of Economic Perspectives* 31 (3): 131–50.

Aggarwal, R., I. Erel, M. Ferreira, and P. Matos. 2011. "Does Governance Travel around the World? Evidence from Institutional Investors." *Journal of Financial Economics* 100 (1): 154–81.

Aggarwal, R., I. Erel, R. Stulz, and R. Williamson. 2009. "Differences in Governance Practices between US and Foreign Firms: Measurement, Causes, and Consequences." *Review of Financial Studies* 22 (8): 3131–69.

Aghion, P., J. Van Reenen, and L. Zingales. 2013. "Innovation and Institutional Ownership." *American Economic Review* 103 (1): 277–304.

Aguilera, R.V., V.J. Bermejo, J. Capapé, and V. Cuñat. 2019. "Firms' Reaction to Changes in the Governance Preferences of Active Institutional Owners." Working paper (13 September). Available at https://papers.ssrn.com/sol3/papers.cfm?abstract_id=3411566.

Albuquerque, R., Y. Koskinen, and C. Zhang. 2019. "Corporate Social Responsibility and Firm Risk: Theory and Empirical Evidence." *Management Science* 65 (10): 4451–69.

Alexander, C.R., M.A. Chen, D.J. Seppi, and C.S. Spatt. 2010. "Interim News and the Role of Proxy Voting Advice." *Review of Financial Studies* 23 (12): 4419–54.

Amel-Zadeh, A., and G. Serafeim. 2018. "Why and How Investors Use ESG Information: Evidence from a Global Survey." *Financial Analysts Journal* 74 (3): 87–103.

Appel, I.R., T.A. Gormley, and D.B. Keim. 2016. "Passive Investors, Not Passive Owners." *Journal of Financial Economics* 121 (1): 111–41.

———. 2018. "Standing on the Shoulders of Giants: The Effect of Passive Investors on Activism." *Review of Financial Studies* 32 (7): 2720–74.

Atta-Darkua, V. 2019. "Corporate Ethical Behaviours and Firm Equity Value and Ownership: Evidence from the GPFG's Ethical Exclusions." Working paper, University of Cambridge (20 June). Available at https://papers.ssrn.com/sol3/papers.cfm?abstract_id=3388868.

Azar, J., M.C. Schmalz, and I. Tecu. 2018. "Anticompetitive Effects of Common Ownership." *Journal of Finance* 73 (4): 1513–65.

Baker, M., D. Bergstresser, G. Serafeim, and J. Wurgler. 2018. "Financing the Response to Climate Change: The Pricing and Ownership of U.S. Green Bonds." Working paper (13 November). Available at https://papers.ssrn.com/sol3/papers.cfm?abstract_id=3275327.

Baldauf, M., L. Garlappi, and C. Yannelis. 2019. "Does Climate Change Affect Real Estate Prices? Only If You Believe in It." Working paper (4 September). Available at https://papers.ssrn.com/sol3/Papers.cfm?abstract_id=3240200.

Barber, B.M., A. Morse, and A. Yasuda. 2019. "Impact Investing." Working paper (12 December). Available at https://papers.ssrn.com/sol3/papers.cfm?abstract_id=2705556.

Bauer, R., T. Ruof, and P. Smeets. 2020. "Get Real! Individuals Prefer More Sustainable Investments." Working paper (25 February). Available at https://papers.ssrn.com/sol3/papers.cfm?abstract_id=3287430.

Bebchuk, L., A. Cohen, and A. Ferrell. 2009. "What Matters in Corporate Governance?" *Review of Financial Studies* 22 (2): 783–827.

Bebchuk, L., A. Cohen, and S. Hirst. 2017. "The Agency Problems of Institutional Investors." *Journal of Economic Perspectives* 31: 89–102.

Bebchuk, L., A. Cohen, and C. Wang. 2013. "Learning and the Disappearing Association between Governance and Returns." *Journal of Financial Economics* 108 (2): 323–48.

Bebchuk, L., and A. Hamdani. 2009. "The Elusive Quest for Global Governance Standards." *University of Pennsylvania Law Review* 157 (5): 1263–317.

Bebchuk, L., and S. Hirst. 2019. "Index Funds and the Future of Corporate Governance: Theory, Evidence, and Policy." *Columbia Law Review* 119 (8): 2029–146.

Becht, M., P. Bolton, and A. Röell. 2003. "Corporate Governance and Control." In *Handbook of the Economics of Finance*, vol. 1, Part A. Edited

59

by George M. Constantinides, Milton Harris, René M. Stulz, 1–109. Amsterdam: Elsevier.

Becht, M., J. Franks, C. Mayer, and S. Rossi. 2009. "Returns to Shareholder Activism: Evidence from a Clinical Study of the Hermes UK Focus Fund." *Review of Financial Studies* 22 (8): 3093–129.

Becht, M., J. Franks, J. Grant, and H.F. Wagner. 2017. "Returns to Hedge Fund Activism: An International Study." *Review of Financial Studies* 30 (9): 2933–71.

Bena, J., M.A. Ferreira, P. Matos, and P. Pires. 2017. "Are Foreign Investors Locusts? The Long-Term Effects of Foreign Institutional Ownership." *Journal of Financial Economics* 126 (1): 122–46.

Bénabou, R., and J. Tirole. 2010. "Individual and Corporate Social Responsibility." *Economica* 77 (305): 1–19.

Berg, F., J.F. Koelbel, and R. Rigobon. 2019. "Aggregate Confusion: The Divergence of ESG Ratings." MIT Sloan Research Paper No. 5822-19 (20 August). Available at https://papers.ssrn.com/sol3/papers.cfm?abstract_id=3438533.

Berle, A.A., and G.C. Means. 1932. *The Modern Corporation and Private Property.* San Diego: Harcourt, Brace & World.

Bernstein, A., M.T. Gustafson, and R. Lewis. 2019. "Disaster on the Horizon: The Price Effect of Sea Level Rise." *Journal of Financial Economics* 134 (2): 253–72.

Bertrand, M., and S. Mullainathan. 2003. "Enjoying the Quiet Life? Corporate Governance and Managerial Preferences." *Journal of Political Economy* 111 (5): 1043–75.

Bessembinder, H. 2016. "Frictional Costs of Fossil Fuel Divestment." Working paper, Arizona State University (5 June). Available at https://papers.ssrn.com/sol3/papers.cfm?abstract_id=2789878.

Black, B.S., A.G. De Carvalho, and É. Gorga. 2012. "What Matters and for Which Firms for Corporate Governance in Emerging Markets? Evidence from Brazil (and Other BRIK Countries)." *Journal of Corporate Finance* 18 (4): 934–52.

BlackRock. 2017. "Viewpoint: Index Investing Supports Vibrant Capital Markets" (October).

Blitz, D., and F.J. Fabozzi. 2017. "Sin Stocks Revisited: Resolving the Sin Stock Anomaly." *Journal of Portfolio Management* 44 (1): 105–11.

Bolton, P., M. Despres, L. Awazu Pereira da Silva, F. Samama, and R. Svartzman. 2020. "The Green Swan: Central Banking and Financial Stability in the Age of Climate Change." Bank for International Settlements (January).

Bolton, P., and M.T. Kacperczyk. 2019. "Do Investors Care about Carbon Risk?" Working paper (18 October). Available at https://papers.ssrn.com/sol3/papers.cfm?abstract_id=3398441.

Bolton, P., T. Li, E. Ravina, and H.L. Rosenthal. 2019. "Investor Ideology." Working paper (28 September). Available at https://papers.ssrn.com/sol3/papers.cfm?abstract_id=3119935.

Borgers, A., J. Derwall, K. Koedijk, and J. Ter Horst. 2013. "Stakeholder Relations and Stock Returns: On Errors in Investors' Expectations and Learning." *Journal of Empirical Finance* 22 (June): 159–75.

Brav, A., W. Jiang, and H. Kim. 2015. "Recent Advances in Research on Hedge Fund Activism: Value Creation and Identification." *Annual Review of Financial Economics* 7 (December): 579–95.

Brav, A., W. Jiang, T. Li, and J. Pinnington. 2018. "Picking Friends before Picking (Proxy) Fights: How Mutual Fund Voting Shapes Proxy Contests." Working paper (17 January). Available at https://papers.ssrn.com/sol3/papers.cfm?abstract_id=3101473.

Bubb, R., and E. Catan. 2019. "The Party Structure of Mutual Funds." Working paper (10 March). Available at https://papers.ssrn.com/sol3/papers.cfm?abstract_id=3124039.

Cai, J., J.L. Garner, and R.A. Walkling. 2009. "Electing Directors." *Journal of Finance* 64 (5): 2389–421.

Carney, M. 2015. "Breaking the Tragedy of the Horizon: Climate Change and Financial Stability." Speech given at Lloyd's of London (29 September).

Ceccarelli, M., S. Ramelli, and A.F. Wagner. 2019. "When Investors Call for Climate Responsibility, How Do Mutual Funds Respond?" *PRI Blog* (2 December). www.unpri.org/pri-blog/when-investors-call-for-climate-responsibility-how-do-mutual-funds-respond/5157.article.

CFA Institute. 2015. "Environmental, Social, and Governance Issues in Investing: A Guide for Investment Professionals." www.cfainstitute.org/-/

media/documents/article/position-paper/esg-issues-in-investing-a-guide-for-investment-professionals.ashx.

———. 2018. "Investment Firm of the Future." https://futurefirm.cfainstitute.org/wp-content/uploads/2019/08/Investment-Firm-of-the-Future.pdf.

Chambers, D., E. Dimson, and E. Quigley. 2019. "To Divest or to Engage? A Case Study of Climate-Change Activism." Working paper, University of Cambridge (15 October). Available at https://papers.ssrn.com/sol3/papers.cfm?abstract_id=3464027.

Chatterji, A.K., R. Durand, D.I. Levine, and S. Touboul. 2016. "Do Ratings of Firms Converge? Implications for Managers, Investors and Strategy Researchers." *Strategic Management Journal* 37 (8): 1597–614.

Chava, S. 2014. "Environmental Externalities and Cost of Capital." *Management Science* 60 (9): 2223–47.

Cheema-Fox, A., B.R. LaPerla, G. Serafeim, D. Turkington, and H.S. Wang. 2019. "Decarbonization Factors." Working paper (18 November). Available at https://papers.ssrn.com/sol3/papers.cfm?abstract_id=3448637.

Cheng, I.H., H. Hong, and K. Shue. 2013. "Do Managers Do Good with Other People's Money?" NBER Working Paper No. w19432 (16 September). Available at https://papers.ssrn.com/sol3/papers.cfm?abstract_id=2325805.

Chowdhry, B., S.W. Davies, and B. Waters. 2019. "Investing for Impact." *Review of Financial Studies* 32 (3): 864–904.

Christensen, H.B., L. Hail, and C. Leuz. 2019. "Adoption of CSR and Sustainability Reporting Standards: Economic Analysis and Review." European Corporate Governance Institute Finance Working Paper No. 623/2019 (9 August). Available at https://papers.ssrn.com/sol3/papers.cfm?abstract_id=3427748.

Claessens, S., and B.B. Yurtoglu. 2013. "Corporate Governance in Emerging Markets: A Survey." *Emerging Markets Review* 15 (June): 1–33.

Coates, J. 2018. "The Future of Corporate Governance Part I: The Problem of Twelve." Harvard Public Law Working Paper No. 19-07 (20 September). Available at https://papers.ssrn.com/sol3/papers.cfm?abstract_id=3247337.

Cole, S., V. Gandhi, and C.L.R. Brumme. 2018. *Background Note: Introduction to Investing for Impact.* Boston: Harvard Business Publishing.

Cremers, M., and A. Ferrell. 2014. "Thirty Years of Shareholder Rights and Firm Value." *Journal of Finance* 69 (3): 1167–96.

Cronqvist, H., and F. Yu. 2017. "Shaped by Their Daughters: Executives, Female Socialization, and Corporate Social Responsibility." *Journal of Financial Economics* 126 (3): 543–62.

Daines, R.M., I.D. Gow, and D.F. Larcker. 2010. "Rating the Ratings: How Good Are Commercial Governance Ratings?" *Journal of Financial Economics* 98 (3): 439–61.

Davis, G.F., and E.H. Kim. 2007. "Business Ties and Proxy Voting by Mutual Funds." *Journal of Financial Economics* 85 (2): 552–70.

Denes, M.R., J.M. Karpoff, and V.B. McWilliams. 2017. "Thirty Years of Shareholder Activism: A Survey of Empirical Research." *Journal of Corporate Finance* 44: 405–24.

Denis, D.K., and J.J. McConnell. 2003. "International Corporate Governance." *Journal of Financial and Quantitative Analysis* 38 (1): 1–36.

Denis, D.K., J.J. McConnell, A.V. Ovtchinnikov, and Y. Yu. 2003. "S&P 500 Index Additions and Earnings Expectations." *Journal of Finance* 58 (5): 1821–40.

Dennis, P.J., K. Gerardi, and C. Schenone. 2019. "Common Ownership Does Not Have Anti-Competitive Effects in the Airline Industry." Working paper (14 August). Available at https://papers.ssrn.com/sol3/papers.cfm?abstract_id=3063465.

Di Giuli, A., and L. Kostovetsky. 2014. "Are Red or Blue Companies More Likely to Go Green? Politics and Corporate Social Responsibility." *Journal of Financial Economics* 111 (1): 158–80.

Dimson, E., O. Karakas, and X. Li. 2015. "Active Ownership." *Review of Financial Studies* 28 (12): 3225–68.

———. 2019. "Coordinated Engagements." Working paper (30 October). Available at https://papers.ssrn.com/sol3/papers.cfm?abstract_id=3209072.

Dunn, J., S. Fitzgibbons, and L. Pomorski. 2018. "Assessing Risk through Environmental, Social, and Governance Exposures." *Journal of Investment Management* 16 (1): 4–17.

Dyck, A., K.V. Lins, L. Roth, and H.F. Wagner. 2019. "Do Institutional Investors Drive Corporate Social Responsibility? International Evidence." *Journal of Financial Economics* 131 (3): 693–714.

Edmans, A. 2011. "Does the Stock Market Fully Value Intangibles? Employee Satisfaction and Equity Prices." *Journal of Financial Economics* 101 (3): 621–40.

———. 2014. "Blockholders and Corporate Governance." *Annual Review of Financial Economics* 6 (1): 23–50.

Edmans, A., and C.G. Holderness. 2017. "Blockholders: A Survey of Theory and Evidence." In *The Handbook of the Economics of Corporate Governance* (Vol. 1), edited by Benjamin Hermalin and Michael Weisbach, 541–636. Amsterdam: North-Holland.

Edmans, A., L. Li, and C. Zhang. 2017. "Employee Satisfaction, Labor Market Flexibility, and Stock Returns around the World." European Corporate Governance Institute Finance Working Paper No. 433/2014 (21 February). Available at https://papers.ssrn.com/sol3/papers.cfm?abstract_id=2461003.

Eichholtz, P., N. Kok, and J.M. Quigley. 2010. "Doing Well by Doing Good? Green Office Buildings." *American Economic Review* 100 (5): 2492–509.

———. 2013. "The Economics of Green Building." *Review of Economics and Statistics* 95 (1): 50–63.

Eichholtz, P., N. Kok, and E. Yonder. 2012. "Portfolio Greenness and the Financial Performance of REITs." *Journal of International Money and Finance* 31 (7): 1911–29.

Engle, R.F., S. Giglio, B.T. Kelly, H. Lee, and J. Stroebel. 2019. "Hedging Climate Change News." CEPR Discussion Paper No. DP13730 (22 May). Available at https://papers.ssrn.com/sol3/papers.cfm?abstract_id=3391077.

European Sustainable Investment Forum. 2018. "European SRI Study."

Fabozzi, F.J., K.C. Ma, and B.J. Oliphant. 2008. "Sin Stock Returns." *Journal of Portfolio Management* 35 (1): 82–94.

Fama, E.F., and K.R. French. 2015. "A Five-Factor Asset Pricing Model." *Journal of Financial Economics* 116 (1): 1–22.

Fender, I., M. McMorrow, V. Sahakyan, and O. Zulaica. 2019. "Green Bonds: The Reserve Management Perspective." *BIS Quarterly Review* (September): 49–63.

Fernandes, N., M.A. Ferreira, P. Matos, and K.J. Murphy. 2013. "Are US CEOs Paid More? New International Evidence." *Review of Financial Studies* 26 (2): 323–67.

Ferreira, M.A., and P. Matos. 2008. "The Colors of Investors' Money: The Role of Institutional Investors around the World." *Journal of Financial Economics* 88 (3): 499–533.

Ferreira, M.A., M. Massa, and P. Matos. 2010. "Shareholders at the Gate? Institutional Investors and Cross-Border Mergers and Acquisitions." *Review of Financial Studies* 23 (2): 601–44.

Flammer, C. 2015. "Does Corporate Social Responsibility Lead to Superior Financial Performance? A Regression Discontinuity Approach." *Management Science* 61 (11): 2549–68.

———. 2019. "Green Bonds: Effectiveness and Implications for Public Policy." NBER Working Paper No. w25950 (17 June). Available at https://papers.ssrn.com/sol3/papers.cfm?abstract_id=3405137.

Freeman, R.E. 1984. *Strategic Management: A Stakeholder Approach.* Cambridge, UK: Cambridge University Press.

French, K.R. 2008. "Presidential Address: The Cost of Active Investing." *Journal of Finance* 63 (4): 1537–73.

Friede, G., T. Busch, and A. Bassen. 2015. "ESG and Financial Performance: Aggregated Evidence from More than 2000 Empirical Studies." *Journal of Sustainable Finance & Investment* 5 (4): 210–33.

Friedman, M. 1970. "The Social Responsibility of Business Is to Increase Its Profits." *New York Times Magazine* (13 September): 173–74.

Geczy, C., J. Jeffers, D.K. Musto, and A.M. Tucker. 2019. "Contracts with (Social) Benefits: The Implementation of Impact Investing." Working paper (9 December). Available at https://papers.ssrn.com/sol3/papers.cfm?abstract_id=3159731.

Gibson, R., S. Glossner, P. Krueger, P. Matos, and T. Steffen. 2019. "Responsible Institutional Investing around the World." Working paper (19 December). Available at https://papers.ssrn.com/sol3/papers.cfm?abstract_id=3525530.

Gibson, R., and P. Krueger. 2018. "The Sustainability Footprint of Institutional Investors." Working paper (15 August). Available at https://papers.ssrn.com/abstract=2918926.

Gibson, R., P. Krueger, N. Riand, and P.S. Schmidt. 2019. "ESG Rating Disagreement and Stock Returns." Working paper (22 December). Available at https://papers.ssrn.com/sol3/papers.cfm?abstract_id=3433728.

Gilje, E., T.A. Gormley, and D. Levit. 2019. "Who's Paying Attention? Measuring Common Ownership and Its Impact on Managerial Incentives."

Journal of Financial Economics (18 December). www.sciencedirect.com/science/article/abs/pii/S0304405X19302934?via%3Dihub.

Gillan, S., and L. Starks. 2003. "Corporate Governance, Corporate Ownership, and the Role of Institutional Investors: A Global Perspective." *Journal of Applied Finance* 13 (2): 4–22.

———. 2007. "The Evolution of Shareholder Activism in the United States." *Journal of Applied Corporate Finance* 19 (1): 55–73.

Gilson, R.J., and J.N. Gordon. 2013. "The Agency Costs of Agency Capitalism: Activist Investors and the Revaluation of Governance Rights." *Columbia Law Review* 113 (4): 863–927.

Giving USA. 2019. "The Annual Report on Philanthropy for the Year 2018."

Global Impact Investing Network. 2019. "The 2019 Annual Impact Investor Survey."

Global Sustainable Investment Alliance. 2019. "Global Sustainable Investment Review for 2018."

Glossner, S. 2017. "ESG Risks and the Cross-Section of Stock Returns." Working paper, University of Virginia Darden School of Business (6 June). Available at https://papers.ssrn.com/sol3/papers.cfm?abstract_id=2980917.

———. 2018. "The Effects of Institutional Investors on Firm Outcomes: Empirical Pitfalls of Quasi-Experiments Using Russell 1000/2000 Index Reconstitutions." Working paper, University of Virginia Darden School of Business (30 May). Available at https://papers.ssrn.com/sol3/papers.cfm?abstract_id=3180776.

———. 2019. "Investor Horizons, Long-Term Blockholders, and Corporate Social Responsibility." *Journal of Banking & Finance* 103 (June): 78–97.

Gompers, P., J. Ishii, and A. Metrick. 2003. "Corporate Governance and Equity Prices." *Quarterly Journal of Economics* 118 (1): 107–56.

Gompers, P.A., and A. Metrick. 2001. "Institutional Investors and Equity Prices." *Quarterly Journal of Economics* 116 (1): 229–59.

Grossman, S.J., and O.D. Hart. 1980. "Takeover Bids, the Free-Rider Problem, and the Theory of the Corporation." *Bell Journal of Economics* 11 (1): 42–64.

Halbritter, G., and G. Dorfleitner. 2015. "The Wages of Social Responsibility—Where Are They? A Critical Review of ESG Investing." *Review of Financial Economics* 26 (1): 25–35.

Hart, O., and L. Zingales. 2017. "Companies Should Maximize Shareholder Welfare Not Market Value." ECGI Finance Working Paper No. 521/2017 (1 October). Available at https://ssrn.com/abstract=3004794.

Hartzmark, S.M., and A.B. Sussman. 2019. "Do Investors Value Sustainability? A Natural Experiment Examining Ranking and Fund Flows." *Journal of Finance* 74 (6): 2789–837.

He, Y., B. Kahraman, and M. Lowry. 2019. "ES Risks and Shareholder Voice." Working paper (26 June). Available at https://papers.ssrn.com/sol3/papers.cfm?abstract_id=3284683.

Heath, D., D. Macciocchi, R. Michaely, and M. Ringgenberg. 2020. "Do Index Funds Monitor?" Working paper (5 March). Available at https://papers.ssrn.com/sol3/papers.cfm?abstract_id=3259433.

Heinkel, R., A. Kraus, and J. Zechner. 2001. "The Effect of Green Investment on Corporate Behavior." *Journal of Financial and Quantitative Analysis* 36 (4): 431–49.

Hoepner, A., I. Oikonomou, B. Scholtens, and M. Schröder. 2016. "The Effects of Corporate and Country Sustainability Characteristics on the Cost of Debt: An International Investigation." *Journal of Business Finance & Accounting* 43 (1–2): 158–90.

Hoepner, A., I. Oikonomou, Z. Sautner, L. Starks, and X. Zhou. 2019. "ESG Shareholder Engagement and Downside Risk." Working paper (31 July). Available at https://ssrn.com/abstract=2874252.

Hong, H., and M. Kacperczyk. 2009. "The Price of Sin: The Effects of Social Norms on Markets." *Journal of Financial Economics* 93 (1): 15–36.

Hong, H.G., G.A. Karolyi, and J. Scheinkman. 2020. "Climate Finance." *Review of Financial Studies* 33 (3): 1011–23.

Hong, H., F.W. Li, and J. Xu. 2019. "Climate Risks and Market Efficiency." *Journal of Econometrics* 208 (1): 265–81.

Hsu, P.-H., K. Li, and C.-Y. Tsou. 2019. "The Pollution Premium." Working paper (8 March). Available at http://gssf.ch/wp-content/uploads/2018/12/The-Pollution-Premium.pdf.

Hsu, P.-H., H. Liang, and P. Matos. 2018. "Leviathan Inc. and Corporate Environmental Engagement." Working paper (30 March). Available at https://papers.ssrn.com/Sol3/papers.cfm?abstract_id=2960832.

Ilhan, E., P. Krueger, Z. Sautner, and L.T. Starks. 2019. "Institutional Investors' Views and Preferences on Climate Risk Disclosure." Working paper (19 August). Available at https://papers.ssrn.com/sol3/papers.cfm?abstract_id=3437178.

Ilhan, E., Z. Sautner, and G. Vilkov. 2020. "Carbon Tail Risk." Working paper, Frankfurt School of Finance and Management (5 March). Available at https://papers.ssrn.com/sol3/Papers.cfm?abstract_id=3204420.

Iliev, P., J. Kalodimos, and M. Lowry. 2018. "Investors' Attention to Corporate Governance." Working paper (27 April). Available at https://papers.ssrn.com/sol3/papers.cfm?abstract_id=3162407.

Investment Company Institute. 2019. "2019 Investment Company Fact Book: A Review of Trends and Activities in the Investment Company Industry." www.ici.org/pdf/2019_factbook.pdf.

IPCC. 2018. "Special Report: Global Warming of 1.5°C: Summary for Policymakers." www.ipcc.ch/site/assets/uploads/sites/2/2019/05/SR15_SPM_version_report_LR.pdf.

Jensen, M.C. 1986. "Agency Costs of Free Cash Flow, Corporate Finance, and Takeovers." *American Economic Review* 76 (2): 323–29.

Jensen, M.C., and W.H. Meckling. 1976. "Theory of the Firm: Managerial Behavior, Agency Costs and Ownership Structure." *Journal of Financial Economics* 3 (4): 305–60.

Khan, M., G. Serafeim, and A. Yoon. 2016. "Corporate Sustainability: First Evidence on Materiality." *Accounting Review* 91 (6): 1697–724.

Kitzmueller, M., and J. Shimshack. 2012. "Economic Perspectives on Corporate Social Responsibility." *Journal of Economic Literature* 50 (1): 51–84.

Kotsantonis, S., and G. Serafeim. 2019. "Four Things No One Will Tell You about ESG Data." *Journal of Applied Corporate Finance* 31 (2): 50–58.

Krueger, P. 2019. "Sustainability Footprinting as a Tool to Implement Mission-Related Investing: How to Use Portfolio-Level Measures of Sustainability to Better Align Investment Strategy and Mission." *Expert Focus* 3: 158–62.

Krueger, P., Z. Sautner, and L.T. Starks. 2020. "The Importance of Climate Risks for Institutional Investors." *Review of Financial Studies* 33 (3): 1067–111.

Krüger, P. 2015. "Corporate Goodness and Shareholder Wealth." *Journal of Financial Economics* 115 (2): 304–29.

Larcker, D.F., A.L. McCall, and G. Ormazabal. 2015. "Outsourcing Shareholder Voting to Proxy Advisory Firms." *Journal of Law & Economics* 58 (1): 173–204.

Larcker, D.F., and E. Watts. 2019. "Where's the Greenium? Stanford School of Business Working Paper (12 February). Available at https://papers.ssrn.com/sol3/papers.cfm?abstract_id=3333847.

Lewellen, K., and M. Lowry. 2019. "Does Common Ownership Really Increase Firm Coordination?" Tuck School of Business Working Paper No. 3336343 (4 March). Available at https://papers.ssrn.com/sol3/papers.cfm?abstract_id=3336343.

Liang, H., and L. Renneboog. 2017. "On the Foundations of Corporate Social Responsibility." *Journal of Finance* 72 (2): 853–910.

Lins, K.V., H. Servaes, and A. Tamayo. 2017. "Social Capital, Trust, and Firm Performance: The Value of Corporate Social Responsibility during the Financial Crisis." *Journal of Finance* 72 (4): 1785–824.

Magill, M., M. Quinzii, and J.C. Rochet. 2015. "A Theory of the Stakeholder Corporation." *Econometrica* 83 (5): 1685–725.

Malenko, N., and Y. Shen. 2016. "The Role of Proxy Advisory Firms: Evidence from a Regression-Discontinuity Design." *Review of Financial Studies* 29 (12): 3394–427.

Masulis, R.W., and S.W. Reza. 2015. "Agency Problems of Corporate Philanthropy." *Review of Financial Studies* 28 (2): 592–636.

Mayer, C. 2013. *Firm Commitment: Why the Corporation Is Failing Us and How to Restore Trust in It*. Oxford, UK: Oxford University Press.

McCahery, J.A., Z. Sautner, and L.T. Starks. 2016. "Behind the Scenes: The Corporate Governance Preferences of Institutional Investors." *Journal of Finance* 71 (6): 2905–32.

McWilliams, A., and D. Siegel. 2001. "Corporate Social Responsibility: A Theory of the Firm Perspective." *Academy of Management Review* 26 (1): 117–27.

Morningstar. 2017. "Passive Fund Providers Take an Active Approach to Investment Stewardship."

———. 2019. "The Evolving Approaches to Regulating ESG Investing."

Murfin, J., and M. Spiegel. 2020. "Is the Risk of Sea Level Rise Capitalized in Residential Real Estate?" *Review of Financial Studies* 33 (3): 1217–55.

Oehmke, M., and M.M. Opp. 2019. "A Theory of Socially Responsible Investment." Swedish House of Finance Research Paper No. 20-2 (21 October). Available at https://papers.ssrn.com/sol3/papers.cfm?abstract_id=3467644.

OECD. 2017. "Investment Governance and the Integration of Environmental, Social and Governance Factors." www.oecd.org/finance/Investment-Governance-Integration-ESG-Factors.pdf.

———. 2019. "Owners of the World's Listed Companies." OECD Capital Market Series (17 October). www.oecd.org/corporate/ca/Owners-of-the-Worlds-Listed-Companies.pdf.

Pastor, L., R.F. Stambaugh, and L.A. Taylor. 2019. "Sustainable Investing in Equilibrium." Working paper (19 December). Available at https://papers.ssrn.com/sol3/papers.cfm?abstract_id=3498354.

Pedersen, L.H., S. Fitzgibbons, and L. Pomorski. 2019. "Responsible Investing: The ESG-Efficient Frontier." Working paper, AQR Capital Management, LLC (18 October). Available at https://papers.ssrn.com/sol3/papers.cfm?abstract_id=3466417.

Pigou, A. 1920. *The Economics of Welfare*. London: Macmillan.

Renneboog, L., J. Ter Horst, and C. Zhang. 2008a. "Socially Responsible Investments: Institutional Aspects, Performance, and Investor Behavior." *Journal of Banking & Finance* 32 (9): 1723–42.

———. 2008b. "The Price of Ethics and Stakeholder Governance: The Performance of Socially Responsible Mutual Funds." *Journal of Corporate Finance* 14 (3): 302–22.

Riedl, A., and P. Smeets. 2017. "Why Do Investors Hold Socially Responsible Mutual Funds?" *Journal of Finance* 72 (6): 2505–50.

Rodrik, D. 2014. "Green Industrial Policy." *Oxford Review of Economic Policy* 30 (3): 469–91.

Schmidt, C., and R. Fahlenbrach. 2017. "Do Exogenous Changes in Passive Institutional Ownership Affect Corporate Governance and Firm Value?" *Journal of Financial Economics* 124 (2): 285–306.

Schramade, W. 2017. "Investing in the UN Sustainable Development Goals: Opportunities for Companies and Investors." *Journal of Applied Corporate Finance* 29 (2): 87–99.

Serafeim, G. 2018. "Investors as Stewards of the Commons?" *Journal of Applied Corporate Finance* 30 (2): 8–17.

Shleifer, A., and R.W. Vishny. 1986. "Large Shareholders and Corporate Control." *Journal of Political Economy* 94 (3, Part 1): 461–88.

———. 1997. "A Survey of Corporate Governance." *Journal of Finance* 52 (2): 737–83.

Smith, A. 1776. *An Inquiry into the Nature and Causes of the Wealth of Nations.* London: W. Strahan and T. Cadell.

Starks, L.T., P. Venkat, and Q. Zhu. 2018. "Corporate ESG Profiles and Investor Horizons." Working paper (23 June). Available at https://papers.ssrn.com/sol3/papers.cfm?abstract_id=3049943.

Statman, M., and D. Glushkov. 2009. "The Wages of Social Responsibility." *Financial Analysts Journal* 65 (4): 33–46.

Strine, L.E., Jr. 2019. "Toward Fair and Sustainable Capitalism: A Comprehensive Proposal to Help American Workers, Restore Fair Gainsharing between Employees and Shareholders, and Increase American Competitiveness by Reorienting Our Corporate Governance System toward Sustainable Long-Term Growth and Encouraging Investments in America's Future." Working paper (11 October). Available at https://papers.ssrn.com/sol3/papers.cfm?abstract_id=3461924.

Sushko, Vladyslav, and Grant Turner. 2018. "The Implications of Passive Investing for Securities Markets." *BIS Quarterly Review* (March): 113–31.

US SIF Foundation. 2018. "Report on US Sustainable, Responsible and Impact Investing Trends 2018."

Wei, W., and A. Young. 2019. "Selection Bias or Treatment Effect? A Re-Examination of Russell 1000/2000 Index Reconstitution." Working paper (23 October). Available at https://papers.ssrn.com/sol3/papers.cfm?abstract_id=2780660.

World Economic Forum. 2019. "The Global Risks Report 2019: 14th Edition." www3.weforum.org/docs/WEF_Global_Risks_Report_2019.pdf.

Yang, R. 2019. "What Do We Learn from Ratings about Corporate Social Responsibility (CSR)?" Columbia Business School Research Paper No. 18-37 (3 December). Available at https://papers.ssrn.com/sol3/Papers.cfm?abstract_id=3165783.

Yermack, D. 2006. "Flights of Fancy: Corporate Jets, CEO Perquisites, and Inferior Shareholder Returns." *Journal of Financial Economics* 80 (1): 211–42.

———. 2010. "Shareholder Voting and Corporate Governance." *Annual Review of Financial Economics* 2 (1): 103–25.

Zerbib, O.D. 2019. "The Effect of Pro-Environmental Preferences on Bond Prices: Evidence from Green Bonds." *Journal of Banking & Finance* 98 (January): 39–60.

Zingales, L. 2015. "Presidential Address: Does Finance Benefit Society?" *Journal of Finance* 70 (4): 1327–63.

Named Endowments

The CFA Institute Research Foundation acknowledges with sincere gratitude the generous contributions of the Named Endowment participants listed below.

Gifts of at least US$100,000 qualify donors for membership in the Named Endowment category, which recognizes in perpetuity the commitment toward unbiased, practitioner-oriented, relevant research that these firms and individuals have expressed through their generous support of the CFA Institute Research Foundation.

Ameritech
Anonymous
Robert D. Arnott
Theodore R. Aronson, CFA
Asahi Mutual Life Insurance Company
Batterymarch Financial
   Management
Boston Company
Boston Partners Asset Management,
   L.P.
Gary P. Brinson, CFA
Brinson Partners, Inc.
Capital Group International, Inc.
Concord Capital Management
Dai-Ichi Life Insurance Company
Daiwa Securities
Mr. and Mrs. Jeffrey Diermeier
Gifford Fong Associates
Investment Counsel Association
   of America, Inc.
Jacobs Levy Equity Management
John A. Gunn, CFA
John B. Neff, CFA
Jon L. Hagler Foundation
Long-Term Credit Bank of Japan, Ltd.
Lynch, Jones & Ryan, LLC
Meiji Mutual Life Insurance
   Company

Miller Anderson & Sherrerd, LLP
Nikko Securities Co., Ltd.
Nippon Life Insurance Company of
   Japan
Nomura Securities Co., Ltd.
Payden & Rygel
Provident National Bank
Frank K. Reilly, CFA
Salomon Brothers
Sassoon Holdings Pte. Ltd.
Scudder Stevens & Clark
Security Analysts Association
   of Japan
Shaw Data Securities, Inc.
Sit Investment Associates, Inc.
Standish, Ayer & Wood, Inc.
State Farm Insurance Company
Sumitomo Life America, Inc.
T. Rowe Price Associates, Inc.
Templeton Investment Counsel Inc.
Frank Trainer, CFA
Travelers Insurance Co.
USF&G Companies
Yamaichi Securities Co., Ltd.

Senior Research Fellows
Financial Services Analyst Association

For more on upcoming Research Foundation publications and webcasts, please visit www.cfainstitute.org/en/research/foundation.

Printed in Poland
by Amazon Fulfillment
Poland Sp. z o.o., Wrocław

65271014R00047